BLACK GYPSY

My Self-Discovery on an Adventure across
France, Egypt, Bahrain, Thailand, and Laos

SHAWNA SHAREE

Cover Photograph by: Anthu Omar

Cover Design: JD Cover Design

www.ShawnaSharee.com

Dedication:

This memoir is dedicated to my first soul mate,
My Mother.

The definition of resilience, compassion, and love.

I'm pretty sure before I incarnated into this world -
I looked through a million options in the universe's
catalog of possible mothers, searching and looking...
Then I spotted you and said "that's her!"

Contents

Acknowledgements

Mom: Thank you for being my biggest cheerleader (soccer Mom), best friend, biggest supporter, and always allowing me to authentically be me. I wouldn't have had the courage to make my dreams into a reality, including this book, if not for you. My creative brain is a creature in itself, thanks for dealing with all my dramatics.

Regina: The Meredith Grey to my Christina Yang. Everyone should have a *Regina* in their life. This is OUR book because it literally wouldn't exist if you weren't in my corner for every twist and turn throughout the 27 years we've spent as friends, especially during this book writing adventure. Words can't describe how much you mean to me.

Kim: You kept me sane during the second half of this process. Thanks for keeping me focused on the goal line, hyping me up, and being my push when my inner pull wasn't kicking in.

Elijah: I wouldn't have started or finished without your presence in my life. From your "you better be writing" text, to just watching you be great. Iron sharpens iron. "Burn the boats!" I appreciate you.

Anthu Omar: Who knew when we ran across the island, Koh Lipe, to chase the sunset, the picture you took of me would end up on the cover of the book I had no clue I'd be writing. Thank you!

Tiffany, Aunt Gwen, Darian, Jason: Thanks for the various ways you continuously checked in to make sure I stayed on point

Mylinda: You challenge me (with everything *rolls eyes*) and make me dig deeper within myself. When I was in Colombia, freaking out, you asked me the right questions to help me make the final decision to write this. Twin senses are real. *wink*

Mrs. Parshall: Thanks for your tough love, critiques, and finding my blind spots — if folks could only read your notes they'd think you were a comedian. I specifically requested to be transferred into your English class in my senior year because I heard how hard and amazing your class was. I had no clue it would be something I'd utilize a decade and a half later.

Kaylee Robinson: My angel beta reader. Your feedback was crucial in helping this book become what it is. You pushed me in the way I needed with your thoughtful, insightful, and straightforward notes.

Amanda: I literally searched high and low for the perfect editor and finally found you. You polished my memoir up (because Lord knows I overuse commas) while changing as little as possible. My fairy Godmother.

My Mastermind: You girls allowed me to clear out my crazy brain every couple of weeks and gave me the accountability I needed. Thank you!

Jubril Agoro, Indigo Ocean, and Stephanie Synclair - The 3 people that look like me, came from places similar to mine, and expanded my view on long term soulful travel. I wrote this book partially because seeing you guys inspired me to take the leap, and I thought I should pay it forward…

Writing a book (and everything that comes along with it after) is much harder than I anticipated. The above people are just the people that helped me through this particular process. There are countless other people I have to acknowledge for being lights and pillars in my life in various ways at different times. I literally have the best family and friends in the world, and could take up an entire book thanking them individually. You know who you are.

Note From The Author

Although this is my personal story and memoir, I wrote it in hopes that you will see yourself through it. I'm a private person by nature — but if my story inspires just one person to believe in themselves, their inner-knowing, and their dreams, it was worth telling.

To thank you for sharing in my adventure and journey, I have a special surprise waiting for you: Free access to some exclusive behind the scene pictures, videos, and even a special video chat with me, talking about what I learned during my first solo trip around the world.

Go to:

www.Black-Gypsy.com

Follow me on

Instagram @ShawnaSharee

…so we can stay connected.

1

FORK IN THE ROAD

I chose my own fate. I drove by the fork in the road and went straight.

~Jay-Z

As I stared at my luggage, I realized I was homeless.

In my sweaty palm, I clutched five pieces of paper that would forever change my life. They weren't even big pieces of paper. No unique embellishments or fun colors. Though small, with predictable type on them, they were my tickets to freedom. I had exchanged my stable life and home for these pieces of paper that were one-way tickets across three continents and five countries to places I'd only dreamed of previously. The terrifying part? Not one of these tickets was a return flight back to the United States of America. I was in the chilly airport yet sweating because I was departing on a journey with no determined end date.

I exhaled, reminiscing about the events that had led me to this moment. Here I was, a black chick who grew up in the Glenn Hazel Housing projects in Pittsburgh, Pennsylvania — the best projects on the planet, might I add — before moving to a middle class neighborhood in middle school. *That* girl was about to globe-trot the world, alone. I didn't come from a lot of money; I worked for everything I had. But what I did have was worth more than gold — the biggest cheerleaders in the world.

My mother programmed me to believe I could do anything. Even now, I can still hear her voice singing the same prayer over me daily my first couple years of life. It sounded like a melodic chant: "I shall be blessed, anything I touch shall prosper, and favor will follow me all of my days." Then there is my stepdad who lights up anytime I come into the room; he taught me how to change tires and car oil, but by example showed me I should never have to. Growing up, I had a close family and extended family friends who were confident that I could do whatever I wanted in this big world. I was crazy enough to believe them.

These folks were used to my wild ideas and big dreams. I hosted and promoted shows in my grandmother's backyard, charging a dollar entrance fee when I was seven. By the time I was thirty-three, nothing that came out of my mouth really shocked them. That is... until I told them I was leaving to travel to Europe, Africa, and Asia by myself.

I had already traveled around the world through books, documentaries, movies, and daydreams. When I was young, my dad would take me to museums and historical sites where I'd get full dissertations on various subjects, especially when we would visit Washington, DC. My love for museums carried into my teenage years. You'd find me at the Carnegie Museum at least once a month, right down the street from my beloved Schenley High School. I would devour the many exhibits but always made my way to the Walton Hall of Ancient Egypt. Observing the artifacts, admiring the mummy they housed behind the glass wall I wanted to pierce through, and imagining what ancient Egypt was like played like a movie in my head on a continuous loop. No matter how many times, it never got old. It was finally my chance in 2015 to have tactile experiences and feel the energy of these places first-hand.

There was only one word to describe what I was feeling before boarding that plane: énouement. The bitter-sweetness of having arrived in the future and not being able to tell your past self how everything unfolds.

You see, I could write a movie that would play on the Lifetime channel about the things that transpired leading up to me traveling the world. I'm going to leave out most of the details, giving you the bare bones so we can get to the good stuff. But it's important that you know it was in my darkest moments that I saw the light. Not an external light, but a light within. When I tuned into it, I realized that I'd had the answers all along.

Twenty-Two Months Before the Grand Exit

I was being fed lies as smooth as the sweet organic maple syrup gliding down my throat, dripping from my favorite pancakes, not knowing it was laced with poison. My on-again-off-again boyfriend for the last decade, Kamau, was in town for the weekend and pleaded his case for us to "make things right" over breakfast. We were headed to Hawaii for my birthday in ten days, and I was in denial, knowing it was supposed to be the end of the end. I forced myself to believe his declarations *this* time. I told myself this conversation was different than the others we had had, so I should give things another fair shot.

I mean, this was the man who had helped me become the go-getter I am and had been one of my greatest teachers up to that point. Anything he wanted to achieve, he figured out a way to make it happen, and he taught me everything he knew about getting things accomplished. Being around that level of ambition every day and mixing that with my strategy skills lit my fire in a way I could never repay him for. I always joked that it was as if he was preparing me to take over the world, even without him in case he died. Well, Sunday November 17, 2013 was *that day* he had been preparing me for metaphorically.

I dropped him off at the airport after having an amazing weekend, but something felt completely off in my gut the entire time. I didn't know what it was exactly, I just knew the agitating whisper wasn't departing, and it made me uneasy.

Then I got my answer. An hour into his flight, I received that email no woman wants to receive, from a young lady "coming to me like a woman," letting me know she had been sleeping with him. I was reading the contents as the air left my lungs, my stomach was dropping, and my chest was getting tighter and tighter. My blood was boiling! I couldn't address or question him because he wouldn't be able to receive calls for another three hours until his flight landed. She waited until she knew he'd be en route, which was clever on her part and a blessing in disguise.

Knowing that every single word that I was deciphering was true but in complete shock, I took a moment and regained my composure. I was ready to explode. To make matters worse, this was happening the day before I was starting a new position at a substantial increase in pay and for which I needed to be 10/10.

I was angry, devastated, hurt, and at the same time... relieved. I had not followed my instincts. Instead I had ignored the whispers telling me this relationship had served its purpose years ago. I turned a deaf ear to the signs when they came in regular tones, telling me to trust my gut. Now the universe had no choice but to scream it at me clear as day to get my attention. *GET OUT!* I was now at full attention like a soldier reporting for duty. The mirror was in my face and on the magnified side. She knew about me the entire time, but I chose not to focus on either her or him. This was about *me*. Someone had to hand me the scissors on a silver platter to cut the cord and get me off autopilot. The autopilot of being comfortable and doing what was safe in every area of my life.

I digested my ego's need for confrontation, even though my chest was still tight and I was aching to speak my piece. *Do not engage*, I thought to myself.

Chess not checkers. I simply forwarded him her email and let him know I would be going to Hawaii alone. I needed boundaries, so I cut off all contact and start trying to make sense of it all.

I felt a piece of me dying a slow and painful death. For some reason it felt freeing and liberating; an energetic disease was exiting my body through the pain. I was aware and knew that the pain I was experiencing, which felt so intense in that moment, would eventually dissolve. I gave myself permission to feel it all with no judgment. Every single range of emotion that naturally came up, I allowed to cycle through my being, and I simply acknowledged it. I had housed the trauma of lies making me think I had crazy illusions made up in my head. But now I could clearly smell the odor of infected flesh that represented those lies, turning into death, finally. I didn't open the window, I allowed the stench to fill the air so I'd always remember it, and one day appreciate it. I told myself I'd visit the graveyard whenever I needed to be reminded that I am connected to the universe in such a way that I should never question it when it tells me something.

Stay soft, I told myself. *But take no shit!*

There was no escaping the fact that living off the fumes of a past reality that no longer fueled any part of me was a recipe where I'd eventually run out of gas if I didn't fill up. I had to fill up. There was a reason I never wanted to marry him or move across the country when he got a promotion, even when he would bring it up. But something about the familiarity kept me rooted in a previous version of myself, even though internally I was not the same person.

Kamau felt safe, but then I asked myself, *what is safety, really?* In this case it was just a mask for my own fear.

I didn't want to hold resentment, so I decided to forgive him in that moment. I reminded myself that he is living out his own human experience, and he has lessons he has to learn as well as his own karma to live out and pay. I needed to figure out what in me needed healing that allowed me to stay with someone far past the expiration date. We were no longer aligned in a variety of ways that had nothing to do with the actual particulars of this circumstance.

I wondered, *why did I choose to stay somewhere where the depths of my soul couldn't be seen? What am I afraid of?* I looked at this relationship as a mirror, no matter how much I wanted to believe Kamau was at fault. There was something in me that attracted this situation to teach and expose things within me that couldn't be exposed any other way. We don't get to decide if we learn the lessons we need; the universe will make sure of it. We only get to choose how many times we have to get the same lesson, even in different situations, before we learn. So I took personal responsibility and did not become a victim.

As I began my exploration, I uncovered my subconscious belief that I had to earn love. I believed I was only worthy of that which I could earn. And what better way to earn love than healing a hurting person? I thought if I squeezed enough, I could get apple juice from an orange. Eureka! That was a breakthrough.

Throughout the years, constantly exposing myself to emotional and energetic toxicity was a violent act upon myself, not a noble one.

I realized I had been in a toxic relationship... *with myself.*

A small piece of freedom was on the other side.

By killing this piece of myself, it meant every other area in my life was now fair game for an audit and reinvention. Everything was an illusion. I was broken open. Being open was the only way I could receive.

The Day After

On my way into my new position the next morning, I knew it would be a test. I was peering at life in a new way. Nothing was safe or off limits. I gave myself permission to change my mind about whatever I wanted, even if that meant making irresponsible decisions.

I had built a cookie-cutter life, working the same job for eight years, living without a *Hell yes!* in sight. My attitude had been, *Oh, that's kinda cool*, and it reflected in my kind of dope but nowhere-near-magical existence that I knew was available for me. I would only take big leaps from now on, and I would learn to be okay with being uncomfortable. The universe knew it had to pull the rug from under my feet, and now I had the figurative blue and black marks to prove the fall.

I sashayed into my new position like I owned the world. It was a job I could do in my sleep—and that was actually problematic with my new zest for life. By the time Thursday rolled around, I felt stuck in a web of complacency, and the question kept entering my mind, *Am I settling?* My new director felt my unease all week. He had just spent the last two months convincing me to take the job, so he was trying to make everything as utopian as possible. It didn't matter. Now that I was awakened in a new way, I knew I was not where I was supposed to be.

Friday arrived, and I was listening to a Wayne Dyer talk on my way to work as I sometimes did. He was telling the ancient South Indian monkey trap story that I had heard a hundred times before.

The tale goes, when the villagers wanted to trap a monkey, they would get a coconut and cut a hole in the shell, hollowing it out precisely big enough for the monkey to put his hand in and out without any problem. They would then put rice inside the coconut and tie it to a stake, knowing the monkey would put his hand inside to grab some rice. With the monkey's hand full of rice, he would struggle and struggle to get his balled fist back out of the precisely-cut hole that was only big enough for him to remove his hand if it were empty.

At any point, if he let go of the rice, the monkey would have no problem removing his hand and getting away. Even knowing someone was coming, and that he might be in danger, instead of letting go of the rice and easily removing his hand to run, he would not let go! The monkey was under no physical restraints... only mental ones. He couldn't, or better put *wouldn't*, leave the rice, even if it cost him his life. He was so tied to the idea of having the rice, he wouldn't drop it. That's how the trap worked perfectly every time.

I had a come to Jesus, Buddha, Muhammad, Krishna, and Osiris moment as it dawned on me that I had just let go of the rice in my left hand and dropped the coconut when I cut contact with Kamau, but I still had a fistful of rice in my right hand stuck in another coconut: More money and this job.

I was a college counselor who poured my soul into pulling out the greatness, dreams, and potential of my students. Fixing things, putting out fires, addressing logistics, remaining inspirational when I was having a bad day, and getting others to tap into their deep-seated dreams are skills I mastered in those eight years. The problem was, I had gotten complacent and wasn't tapping into my own dreams as I inspired thousands of others to do. I had gotten comfortable. From the outside looking in, my life was pretty damn good. By society's standards, I should've been happy; I was right on par with checking off all the hallmarks of being "successful." I had strived my entire life to get what I wanted and always had the mentality that I could figure everything out. *So why was I settling now?*

"The lust for comfort murders the passions of the soul," wrote Kahlil Gibran. This was not the life I wanted to live, and having given myself permission to be reckless, I quit my job that day and figuratively dropped the rice. The second I got my right hand out of that coconut, I literally threw up the deuces with my newly freed fingers. I got several calls and emails from the director trying to convince me to stay, but my mind was made up. No rice-money was worth me not living my best life. I was starting an internal revolution.

My birthday trip to Hawaii was a few days away, which was exactly what I needed. I couldn't wait to get away from everything I had just quit, which seemed like my entire life as I knew it.

2

DARK NIGHTS IN HAWAIIAN PARADISE

I pack up all my sins and I wear them to the show, and let 'em go let 'em go let 'em go let 'em go…

~Jay Electronica

Entering my hotel room alone, I dropped my bags and immediately opened the sliding glass doors that led to the balcony overlooking the ocean. My breath was taken away as the sounds of the waves crashed onto the shore. The aroma of the ocean filled my nose as I walked out, immediately captivated by my surroundings. It all finally hit me. I braced the chair and took a seat as the evening sky haunted me with its stillness, inducing the adrenaline to finally wear off.

For the first time, I was able to truly process what had happened without any external stimuli. I was traumatized and in complete shock. I had no job, and no boyfriend: Two things I hadn't been without in my adult life.

What the hell have I done? What am I going to do now? Why would I quit my job? How could I be so stupid? I let myself feel it all, then slowly moved into the even scarier thought—for the first time in a long time, I could do whatever I wanted. Which meant now I had to figure out what it was I desired, come up with a plan, and let God fill in the blanks.

I knew for sure at that point in my life that all I had to do was keep following the trail of breadcrumbs and remain curious.

After twenty minutes in silence, letting my anxiety make its rounds, I start contemplating what my dream life would feel like down in my bones, if I had no limitations, no outside judgment, and unlimited resources. Not in a superficial way. I wrote down how I wanted to feel, what I dreamed of doing, who I wanted to be in the world, how I wanted to love and be loved. I even thought about what life would taste, sound, and smell like if I just had a blank canvas. It felt empowering with the ever-expansive ocean as my backdrop, representing the free-flowing life I craved. *Be strong yet flexible like water*, I thought. A new level of excitement replaced my previous gloom.

I knew before I could live out the life I wanted, I had to change my current reality. I mean, dreams aren't free.

The good thing was, I had been investing my money, and I mean thousands and thousands of dollars, into digital marketing courses for the previous two years. I had made many sacrifices, from not buying shoes when I wanted, not eating out, not going on trips, and instead putting my money into learning and saving. I knew I had the tools and the brains to make anything happen, and I had already started building a digital business. Now I just had to follow through. I decided to stop the worry train and just enjoy my time in paradise, which was the perfect place to detox from my old life.

During my time alone in Hawaii, I hiked to waterfalls, rode ATVs, went horseback riding, read on the beach, talked for hours with many strangers, and enjoyed every second of it. It was at that moment I realized I loved solo travel much more than I knew. I didn't have to consult anyone about what we were going to do that day, which meant I could spend ten minutes looking at a tree if I wanted, or wake up and dance around naked at 3:00 a.m. Most importantly, it meant I could see the world through my eyes, on my time, at my pace.

My best friend, Regina, was getting married on the island a week after my solo adventure, which is why I had gone a week early for my birthday in the first place. By the time they got there, I was refreshed and invigorated. I had the time of my life witnessing my best friend since age ten marry her Action Figure, our nickname for him.

***

When I got back home from Hawaii, I made the decision to finally start traveling long-term. *I should be ready to travel the world in three to four months*, I thought. Ha! That's the funny thing about making plans. Little did I know, a complete storm was brewing. My grandmother got really sick, and being I "had no real job," I became the one to take care of her. At that point, I was taking care of everyone else, not including myself, and a year and a half later, I was completely exhausted. I had enough money saved and enough coming in each month that I was ready to get out of the country and possibly never return. My energy was heavy; I could feel it. I knew I had to leave soon, or I would be stuck.

I had been dreaming of traveling since I read *Eat Pray Love* in 2006, nine years before. This was a couple years after I started down the rabbit hole of true spiritual awakening. Traveling long-term was at the top of my bucket list along with writing a book, but back in 2006, I thought I would have to wait until I was retired or rich to do it. I mean, I wasn't a white woman with money and the means to just up and trot the globe. "That's something privileged white people do," I actually said out loud to myself. My ingrained limited belief let me believe there was a rule that it wasn't possible, when the rule existed only in my mind. As far as I knew, no one where I came from just up and left on an adventure. So I let it remain an item on my bucket list for all those years, thinking I would have to save up a disposable few hundred thousand dollars first, and *then* I could see the world. Still, after I read the book, a part of me was awakened even then, and subconsciously I broke a piece of my agreement with that limited belief.

Now, in 2015, I had the full belief it was possible, I just had to figure out the details. And that's what I did.

3

DAYDREAMS VS. REALITY

It was all a dream. I used to read

WORD UP! Magazine.

~Notorious B.I.G.

I hadn't been a part of any travel groups and didn't have any resources. I didn't have an Instagram account at the time, so I hadn't connected with other travelers. Prancing into this almost blind, I knew I had to put my research skills to use. If there's one thing I am, it's resourceful. Browsing the internet one day, I saw an inexpensive one-way flight from DC to Paris, leaving in less than a month for $230. I didn't think, I just booked it! My original plan was to start out somewhere closer, like Costa Rica, to get my feet wet for a couple of months before I ventured farther away. France was significantly farther. After hitting the "confirm purchase" button, my heart started beating at a rapid pace, and I thought, *I'm leaving in less than a month!*

The wheels in my brain began to rotate... *The flight from Paris to Egypt can't be that expensive – it's right there basically*, I contemplated. I searched, but couldn't find a flight that day in the price range I was looking for. Ironically, what I did find was a flight from Egypt to Abu Dhabi sixteen days later. Like the full-on risk-taker I had become... I booked it! I was now in shock. *Did you just book a flight to Paris and then a flight from Egypt to Abu Dhabi, when you don't have a flight from Paris to Egypt?* As crazy as it was, I knew I was following the breadcrumbs, and my intuition was right. Two days later I found a flight from Paris to Egypt for under $200, which would give me ten days in my dream destination, Egypt.

Paris was an afterthought at that point... all I could think was, *I AM GOING TO KEMET! Is this real life?!* Kemet is one of the original names of Egypt, and it was indeed real life, the life I never thought I'd be able to live until I was sixty. I was going to the land I had spent so much time trying to get close to all those years in the Carnegie Museum.

When I finally got a hold of my mom, she started screaming even more excitedly than me, "Oh my goodness, you're going to have the time of your life! Where to after that?"

It's funny how quickly my paradigm shifted. At this point, I looked at flying to different countries like it was going down the street. The world was my oyster, and my world had already expanded, even if only in my head at that point. I knew I had to visit my best friend, Regina, who had just moved to Bahrain, which was so close to Egypt and Abu Dhabi. Her husband, the Action Figure she'd married in Hawaii, was in the US Navy, and they were recently stationed there. That would have to be another ten- to fourteen-day stop.

Out of the blue I thought, *Thailand! I am supposed to go to Thailand.*

I had seen a Facebook video of a black guy from Chicago, Jubril, in a place called Chiang Mai, Thailand, so I started searching for flights from

Bahrain to Thailand. I also knew Thailand had never been colonized by a European nation, and that made it enticing in itself. I had no idea where I would go after Thailand... my instincts said stop. So, I had a one-way flight to Thailand and no clue what would happen once I got there.

I reflected on my intentions for this adventure. *What do I want to feel and experience?* This was a technique I'd had every one of my students and coaching clients do for the past decade. When they told me they wanted to go to school to make good money, we would dig for the underlying feeling having money would give them because that is what would keep them inspired and going. That feeling is what we are always striving to acquire. No matter how long it took, my students and I would dig until we hit the root of how they wanted to actually feel. The tables were turned. Now it was my turn to do this exercise. It was simple, I wanted to feel... *curious, happy, and free.*

Traveling solo was ideal. I wanted to glimpse the human experience in different places from completely different lenses, not go on a vacation. I was looking for deep immersion. I made the decision to pick apartments in real neighborhoods where I wasn't likely to run into other Americans regularly, squeezing me out of my comfort zone. I figured with very few safety nets, I'd get what I wanted—authentic experiences.

Strategically, I didn't tell a lot of people I was leaving until right before I left. As soon as I did, answering questions about possibly getting kidnapped became the norm. It seemed like everyone's obsession, and it was comical how everyone became an expert on world relations, world travel and world security when I told them I was leaving the country alone. People freely handed out advice, having no real idea of what they were talking about. Most were beyond excited, even through their agonizing concern.

"It must be nice," was the passive-aggressive statement that hit me a few times. I would internally roll my eyes and chuckle, having learned over the years not to take on other people's energy. I simply responded, "Yup! It is nice." The fact that I quit a well-paying job and was going to travel the world seemed ridiculous and unattainable to some. Their opinions were okay with me and quite frankly none of my business.

I had given away most of my belongings and became a minimalist, knowing experiences were more important to me than hanging onto a bunch of things. I had no problem living with very little materially, and since I had no debt, had paid my bills down to my cell phone, insurance premiums, and little stupid things like Netflix and business tools I used, I wasn't worried about what anyone else had to say. I had no kids and no reason to live in anyone else's safe paradigm of how the world is supposed to work. That's the thing I had to remember — people project their own insecurities and fears onto you when you're doing something they want to do but do not have the guts to do. Smile and move on.

My moves were intentional, even if they seemed flaky. I had gotten off auto-pilot, ready to test drive. I was confident and excited!

As the time approached, I decided I would take a small suitcase and my backpack for electronics. I knew it would be best if I could easily lift my suitcase myself and wasn't weighed down by too much. Realizing I had no idea how long I would be gone, packing became a chess match. After some YouTube research, I finally figured out a way to take the equivalent of 20 outfits in my tiny suitcase. That was a win!

My dad drove me to the airport after giving me a small silver whistle to keep with me, preferably around my neck. This was one of the ten whistles he has throughout his house and on every nightstand. He checked to make sure I had downloaded the government Safe Travelers app, and I had. I purposely left out that I was going to Egypt alone, knowing he would have freaked out, being he had been to that region a number of times for work. I got out of the car and started what seemed like a sleep-walk into the airport. In a daze, I only heard, "Be careful," as it finally struck me. I felt numb, thinking, *You're leaving the country and have no idea when you're coming back.*

I had the butterflies I always got right before going on stage during my years as a ballerina. You can't describe it other than the strange combination of excitement and anxiousness to the point you feel like you have to poop. Yup, that was the feeling I had.

I was having an out-of-body experience, but my legs kept gliding towards the airport entrance, then to the counter, through security, and to the gate.

For a moment I regretted not buying a return ticket home. At least then I wouldn't be out there in the world, winging it. But there was no turning back now.

4

BLOOD MOONS OVER PARIS

I'm an orange moon.

Reflecting the light of the sun.

~Erykah Badu

The blood moon was scheduled to appear in the night sky the night of my flight. Luckily it was the exact same time I'd be in the air. I made sure I had a window seat and booked the emergency row for extra room. As I waited at the gate, fear and anxiety started creeping their way in like a sly cat waiting to pounce. *This was really it!* I was about to plant my feet on Europe, Africa, the Middle East, and Asia in the next couple of months, and I had no clue what made me think it was a good idea to do this alone. When I decide to do something, I go from 0 to 100 in a blink of an eye; I don't have an in between.

I began considering the many border controls I was about to encounter, getting from the airports, the possibilities of my phone getting stolen, getting locked up in foreign jail for doing something I didn't know was illegal, and everything else I could imagine. My mind was racing at full speed. I knew to let those emotions roll through without trying to restrict or judge them. I acknowledged them and decided to quickly figure out the root issue, which was: I was embarking on something that was brand new territory, and it was perfectly normal to be nervous. I decided to focus on the planning I had done and all the life-changing experiences I was about to have.

As I boarded my flight to Paris, I took a deep breath and touched the charm bracelet gifted to me by one of my best friends, Kadia, that is engraved with the words, "What's for you will not pass you!" Grabbing it is a habit of mine when I need to calm down and trust myself. I found my seat, sat down, and began looking at all the faces still boarding. None of those faces looked like me, and most of those people were traveling with other people. I was about to fly across the ocean, and not to the Caribbean, where I had been before, but the big ocean, where it would take half a day for anyone to get to me if something happened. A full day once I was in Thailand!

The flight was ready for take-off as the flight attendants made their final checks. This was my last chance. The plane began to roll, bumping up and down on the tarmac as the aircraft accelerated before we were finally off the ground. That's when shit got real!

Hours into the flight, 30,000 feet up in the air, while most were sound asleep, a pretty Irish-looking girl about twenty-six years old found the space right in front of me that was open for emergencies. She sat on the floor, gazing out the window, hoping to catch a glimpse of the rare moon that should have been making its entrance at any moment. We looked at each other and appreciated that there was someone else as excited to witness this super moon moment. The sky was glooming, and now the blood moon was clearly visible. The chances of actually being in the sky during a total lunar eclipse of a super moon was slim to none. This lunar event happened to be the last in a series of four, and the combination was so rare it hadn't occurred since 1967. It would last only one hour and twelve minutes, and we were witnessing it first-hand. In astrology, the harvest moon, as it is also called, is believed to carry the energy for endings. It creates shifts — ending old energy and patterns and jumpstarting transformations. A moon for awakening. It made sense that our paths aligned.

Little did I know, I wouldn't return to the United States for another seven months, and when I returned, I wouldn't be the same person. A version of myself that had served me well up to that point was being left that day, and the evolution would be at an accelerated pace.

The moon was a sign that I had synchronistic surprises awaiting me, the types of coincidences I couldn't coordinate myself if I wanted to. If I paid attention, I'd know there were forces cheering me on, and I was getting my first wink before I even landed.

***

I finally arrived in Paris completely out of it and exhausted. I hadn't slept at all on the plane and was quite nervous about my commute to the rented apartment in the center of the city. My scheduled stay in Paris was pretty brief, just a couple of days. I hoped to get in as much sightseeing as possible.

As I eased through Immigration, I sighed. *That's it*? An exhale left my chest as I thought how I had rehearsed the worst possible scenarios, knowing that 99% of the time they never happen. As I collected my one piece of black luggage that screamed fierce with its intricate, glistening, woven pattern, I start making my way out.

Several men spoke to me in French, but I had no clue what any of them were saying. One in particular was absolutely gorgeous with deep chocolate skin, sultry eyes, and a sexy accent. I didn't have the time to flirt in another language, although I usually always make time to flirt, even with old ladies, but at this point I was on a mission: decide if I was going to take a train, taxi, Uber, or find an inexpensive shuttle bus into the city. I tried to figure out the train line for fifteen minutes, trying to participate in the local thing... but I told myself to take it easy my first day. I splurged on a $50 Uber. I needed food and rest ASAP, plus I didn't want to be late for my first Airbnb experience.

Five minutes after requesting an Uber, I was on the phone with Patrick, who informed me in broken English that I was on the wrong side of the airport. We played tag for ten minutes before finally finding one another; I was relieved. Patrick was a handsome African man who had moved to France as a teenager. He had a big beautiful smile, gorgeous brown skin, and amazing energy. After placing my bag in the trunk, he opened my door like a gentleman. I was off on my first adventure.

We immediately clicked like old friends and started a lively conversation, talking about everything. We discussed where I was coming and going, his family, our favorite music. I found out he loved Missy Elliott, and when I told him I used to be an emcee in my younger days, he insisted I play him some music. I pulled my iPod out of my backpack, and he connected his auxiliary chord into the plug. I scrolled through my music and found an old song of mine that I loved.

As the song played, his eyes quickly became five times their normal size. Suddenly, he started screaming at the top of his lungs, "No waaaaaayyyy, this is you?! You sound famous! I'm in the car with a famous person!"

I began laughing at a level that matched his enthusiasm, which meant we were both at a level 10, feeding off each other even more. Anyone passing us on the road had to think we were on Mars. I was tickled pink at his excitement, but I let him know I was *not* famous and had quit my music hobby years and years ago.

"I think you are lying to me, Shawna. You just don't want me to know you are a star!" he insisted, giving me a serious side-eye, implying I was trying to get one over on him.

My laughter grew even louder as I watched him bobbing back and forth to the drum beat and bass, with which my voice had become another instrument.

Five minutes later, after finally calming down, I found out he assumed I was half white. "When I see you, Shawna, I think you have one parent black and one parent white. Look at your skin!" he stated with all the confidence in the world.

This led to a discussion about the slave trade, Native Americans, and the raping of African slaves by white slave masters. He was hearing ninety percent of these details for the first time, which was interesting. He knew the basics of American slavery, but that was it. It finally made more sense to him how I could have light-colored eyes, be light, have waist-length hair, and not have a white parent, grandparent, or great-grandparent. I thought to myself how far I had grown in this area.

There was a time I would have been extremely irritated at someone thinking I was mixed, let alone possibly white. I have fair skin, with green, blue, or silver eyes, depending on the day, and at that time extremely long hair—all things that are automatically deemed "mixed features." I used to be offended when anyone suggested it. It was something I was insecure about. Growing up predominantly with my mom's side of the family, where I was by far the lightest member, I've always been unapologetically black.

My mom began teaching me black power chants when I was three, and my name was almost Africa until my grandmother talked her out of it. My best friends growing up, other than my godsister, were all dark-skinned or deep brown girls, so the running joke was I was dark-skinned at heart. I longed for my eyes to be brown and my skin to be darker so people would never ask me, "What are you?" I hated when I answered that I'm black, and some would proceed to tell me there's no way I was not mixed. It especially stung coming from the lips of other black people.

There came a point when a friend, whose family and friends called me "Sister Souljah" along with the "Green-Eyed Bandit," told me I needed to stop trying to prove myself and step into my own power.

"The thing that pisses me off about you is you keep searching for the light, not realizing you are the damn light. You don't have to prove a damned thing to anyone. Your energy is so powerful, and you don't even have a clue," he proclaimed, not knowing that

that one thing said by someone who knew me so well triggered something inside me that clicked.

I started embracing and accepting that my "look," which I hated so much in the white America I live in, gave me certain "privileges," and I only call them privileges as they relate to people more melanated than me. No matter how messed up it was, I realized the way I looked was less threatening to some people. Coupled with my bubbly personality (in social situations), this allowed me access and the ears of people in different ways.

Like the time Human Resources held a meeting asking for referrals or ideas for hiring. I stood up and articulated how, in a predominantly white working culture and environment, referrals should not be a main way of seeking new hires, because most likely it would only lead to a bigger pool of people with the same demographics. Everyone was open to hearing and brainstorming suggestions on how to increase diversity. I know that everyone may have been more receptive to it partially because my appearance made me seem less threatening, despite my assertive personality. Not to negate that I was typically outgoing, helpful, with a great work ethic, but I'm sure my "look" made it easier to digest because it made them more comfortable. I'm not sure that was the catalyst, but the hiring numbers of minorities were vastly increased after that meeting.

So when Patrick said what he said, me laughing genuinely and uncontrollably was *huge* progress. When you look for reasons to be offended, you will always find them. Not a single part of me was offended, but instead I saw it as a beautiful opportunity for dialogue with an African brother who had a totally different experience, moving to Paris from the African continent as a teenager. He had no idea of the depth of the slave trade and was extremely curious about my native Nanticoke bloodline as well. In exchange, I learned a great deal about what it was like to be an immigrant in France. The conversation was easy and warm, like talking with an old friend.

We laughed and carried on like old pals for the entire ride, exchanging information when he finally dropped me off. He let me know that he would take me around to hang out if I had the time or anytime I come to Paris. That Uber ride reassured me that this trip would have tons of mini adventures around every corner. I planned to be amazed by them all.

***

The Airbnb host had left the key in a lockbox, needing to leave before I got there. I fussed with the tricky old French lock for about three minutes before the door opened, making a loud squeaking sound as the antiquated studio apartment was revealed. I realized I was indeed in France. The apartment was cold and hollow but had French charm and flare. Once I figured out how to turn the heat up, I felt more cozy. Since I wasn't staying long, I booked a location that was only one block from the Eiffel tower. I showered and put on my signature color, all black: Black tight pants, black shirt, black boots, black vegan leather jacket, and black wooden triangle earrings that hung down, almost touching my shoulder. I rapidly exited the apartment to explore what is said to be one of the most beautiful cities in the world. It was brisk, but the sun was beaming on me like a spotlight. I felt alive and vibrant as I walked down the streets, immediately spellbound by my surroundings. While admiring the gorgeous architecture, I imagined books being written, pianos being played, and the strokes of painters' brushes making art pieces behind each door. I passed a couple of shops, and the smell of freshly baked bread seeped out, making me crave a bite… or fifty. I put on some classical music in my headphones, which reminded me of my hours of ballet training as I pranced my way to the Eiffel Tower after eating. I walked the streets for hours, seeing some more tourist attractions before I was absolutely beat.

That night, as I lay in bed, the breeze from the old window made its way in, causing the glass to rattle. I stared up at the ceiling twelve feet above and whispered to myself, "You're not dreaming—this is real life, Shawty."

***

One of the online courses I had taken had a vibrant 10,000-person Facebook community attached to it. I remembered one of the ladies I adored, Malaika, had lived in Paris for a year. I shot her an email a couple of days before leaving to get a few tips.

She informed me that another member of the community, Mylinda, was in Paris for a couple of months, and she insisted we should meet. Mylinda and I decided we would catch a bite to eat a couple of hours before my departure, near the famous Champs Elysées. I was staying less than two miles away and thought it would be fun to walk. Walking is one of the best ways to get to know a place.

My black suitcase was small enough to pull easily, and my backpack would be a breeze. I felt like I was in a movie, and I heard dramatic music playing in my head as I passed the gorgeous architecture, beautiful streets, and bridges. I was enchanted by everything I saw. It reminded me of Carrie while she was in Paris in the last couple episodes of *Sex and the City*. I was smiling, skipping, and living my best life when I realized I was lost. *How could GPS betray me like this? Where did I make the wrong turn? Why am I walking in a circle? Didn't I just pass this intersection?*

My enchantment quickly turned to frustration. I rang Mylinda, who tried to figure out exactly where I was, but nothing sounded familiar. Forty minutes later, we finally found each other, but at that point, I had only half an hour before I needed to find my shuttle bus to the airport.

We found a café and grabbed some hot drinks, croissants, and other French goodies you're supposed to eat when in France. Her sexy little Australian accent mesmerized me with everything she said. It was eerie — we were basically the same person with the same sense of humor you don't often run across. Granted, she was a good seven inches taller (not with my heels on, though!), white, and a decade older than me. She grew up in a rural area with animals, farms, and lakes. It didn't matter; Mylinda was my long-lost twin.

Time stood still, and we agonized that it was almost time for me to leave. We raced up the street to find the shuttle, which I made just in time.

"Text me when you get through security and then, of course, when you get to Egypt," she insisted.

We embraced, and off I went.

Little did I know I had just met a woman who would become one of my best friends on the planet. There are very few people I talk to daily and even fewer people I talk to when I'm moody or don't want to be bothered. Somehow, this smart-ass Australian girl I met by chance is one of those few I talk to regardless of how I'm feeling. We push each other's buttons like sisters but have instincts between the two of us like twins. I joke all the time that I came to Paris just to meet her, and she jokes that if we were lesbian, we would have the best love story ever. Paris was short and sweet, but I'm convinced I found that cheap ticket and instinctually bought it because Patrick and Mylinda were waiting for me.

I had followed the breadcrumbs and, instead of collecting souvenirs in Paris, I had collected two dope souls.

5

EGYPTIAN VORTEX

The world wonder, I'm still standing like pyramids. Design so vivid, every brick it got a story to tell…

~Rakim

The moment I had been awaiting my entire life was finally here; nothing was going to stop me. Right before I left the States, twelve people, mostly tourists, were killed in Egypt. Tourism had already plummeted in the few years preceding, so not many people were going to Egypt, let alone solo female travelers. My instincts told me I'd be fine; I was going, and going solo.

I have no fear of death. I have a slight fear of the act of dying, as in I don't want to drown or be shot and bleed out... but the thought of not existing in this reality is not something I'm afraid of. I have lived a great life, and if it's my time to go, I'm ready for the next chapter, which I'm sure will be even more exciting. I thought to myself, *if I die, at least I will have died in Egypt! I'm going, unless TuPac appears and tells me not to, and then he'd have to have Bob Marley as his hype man reiterating the message.*

I was hitting the gas pedal full speed as far as solo adventures goes. Paris was only so far out of my comfort zone, but now I would be staying in Giza. Not the tourist Giza—I was staying in a neighborhood where I might not see another traveler or tourist my entire stay. I was in for *major* culture shock.

I hesitantly walked onboard the plane, immediately feeling the difference in energy. Every country has its own energy the people carry. The plane was packed, and everyone was speaking Arabic. Aesthetically speaking, I blended right in. Anyone who spoke to me expected me to speak Arabic. I was modestly dressed, and having been well versed in and around Islamic culture, I felt pretty comfortable. I was still quite aware I was a woman traveling alone, and that the men in modern Egypt can be aggressive, or so I heard. I had read many accounts online of their aggressiveness, but that didn't make me nervous. If worse came to worse, I had a dad, stepdad, and a couple cousins who would find me like Liam Neeson in *Taken*, so I was pretty calm. I like to experience things for myself, not via a second-hand account, so onward and upward it was.

My flight was landing in the middle of the night, at 12:30 a.m. local time. It was probably not the best idea, but it was what it was. We were about an hour out when a flight attendant started passing out the country entry cards that needed to be completed. She accidentally gave me a nationals' card, assuming I was an Egyptian citizen. She questioned herself, taking an extra couple seconds to make sure she was correct. I smiled, shaking my head no, as she smiled and switched it to a foreigners' card, saying in broken English, "You trick me."

Once I made my way off the plane, I followed the foot traffic until I saw where I needed to purchase my visa. I proceeded to the window to exchange some money, then purchased my visa to get through

Immigration. I was slightly nervous during this process; on top of being tired, I was in an extremely foreign place, and it was quite different than landing in Paris, where I just had to get a stamp and was good. After making it through, getting my bag, and charging my phone, I figured out where to meet Yasiin, my Airbnb host for the next week and a half... and soon-to-be adopted big cousin.

***

He spotted me and waved me over as I saw the sign he was holding with my name on it. I walked towards him while he was simultaneously screeching, "NO NO NO NO NO!" I had no idea what was going on at that point or why he looked distressed.

He looked into my eyes and said, "Welcome! I had no idea your face would be so strong, and you would look Egyptian. You are my cousin. Say nothing to no one. My head will hurt worried about you now. This may be problem." As he was telling me to say "nothing to no one," his arms were complementing his seriousness as he gestured "no."

I was still trying to figure out what the heck he meant by saying my face is strong. *Do I look like a man to him?* It was all I could think of. Then, as every male eye gazed at me as we exited the airport, it dawned on me he was expressing that I'm attractive.

The moment my feet hit the ground outside, I snapped out of my thoughts and started smiling from ear to ear... "I'm in Africa! I'm breathing African air," I whispered. A sense of peace descended over me as a warm breeze passed my face in the dry desert heat. In that moment, no matter what happened, it was worth it. I had touched the ground and breathed the air… in Africa.

By this time, it was well after 1:30 a.m. I was exhausted, nervous, and anxious. We had a thirty-plus-minute drive to get to my new neighborhood in Giza, and despite my exhaustion, my eyes were wide open the entire time—because of Yasiin's driving! This was definitely another reality I was not accustomed to. As he maneuvered through the traffic, I thought I was going to die in a car crash at least three times. I couldn't believe this was in the middle of the night. On a five-lane street with cars buzzing by fast, people just crossed the street in the middle of the commotion… They just hoped for the best. He laughed and chuckled every time I gasped or said, "Woooaaahhh."

"I drive long time, my friend, no worry," he tried to reassure me, but it wasn't working.

Yasiin told me about all the programs (places), he can "make for me" (take me), because I should not go anywhere alone. He alerted me there was a teenage boy who lived in the apartment building, a nice boy, and if I ever wanted to leave when he was not around, I should go and get him, Mohammed, or Mohammed's father. They would escort me. At that point I got a little freaked out, but I checked myself and thought, *You ain't no punk.*

We approached a bridge, and as if it were just any little river, Yasiin asked me, "That's the Nile. I can pull over if you want?"

Yes. Yes! And YES again! I thought but didn't say… My eyes must have said it all, because he laughed and pulled over. "We will get out quickly."

There were older men sitting and fishing on the bridge in the wee hours of the morning, looking as content as one can look. I gazed at the river as if it were a time portal. A feeling rushed over me as it sank in. I was staring at *the* Nile River. The river that supplied fertile soil to all the ancient African pharaohs, kings, queens, scientists, astronomers, artists, and great minds of this land. The *great river iteru* that let the ancient people of Egypt know what season it was, made agriculture possible, and ran all the way through Nubia/Sudan, Ethiopia, Uganda, Congo, and so many other important parts of the greatest and richest continent on earth. Here I was, fresh off the airplane experiencing this moment alone — not part of a tour, or with friends, or a lover, just myself and the great Nile I had imagined since I was ten. It was magical.

Yasiin bolted me out of my moment, informing me, "We come back another day, time to go."

I skipped back to the car like the ten-year-old girl who fell in love with Egypt, and I could tell Yasiin was tickled at my excitement, even though he was shaking his head. I think it was at that very moment he knew he had his hands full for the next ten days.

"I will call you Shosho!" he exclaimed.

It was an Egyptian name that he thought sounded close to Shawna. He would introduce me as such, being I was his cousin and all now.

We finally entered the neighborhood I would call home, and I thought to myself, *Man, what exactly did I get myself into? This looks like a movie! I really might die.* The tan, brown, and beige mid-rise buildings, all having five to six levels, looked like they were made out of stone. The sandy dirt roads, the cars—it all made me question if I should have stayed in a hotel. Yasiin kept reiterating to me I was not to leave alone, which made it worse. If I wanted anything, call him or go get Mohammed. He must have sensed I'm hard-headed and stubborn, so he wanted to make sure I got it. He drilled it into my head... *My face was too strong to walk around alone, and nobody will speak English, so it's not a good idea at all. I am his cousin. My name is Shosho.* This would be a time I followed instructions 100%.

My plan before arriving was to assess during the ten days if I felt comfortable enough to go to some of the other places in Egypt alone. I was longing to visit Luxor, Alexandria, and Aswan, since I had enough time. I immediately canceled that out of my mind, figuring I'd do that on another trip when I had someone else with me. I was going to be as smart as possible traveling by myself without sacrificing adventures. I decided I would just enjoy myself in Giza.

Approaching the apartment building after driving through the neighborhood, I felt like I was having another out-of-body experience. I experience fear, but I'm rarely afraid. At this point, I was afraid. *You're definitely not in Kansas anymore*, I thought to myself, and I wasn't quite sure if I was in their version of the 'hood. I took a deep breath looking at the building, and stepped out of the car in what seemed like slow motion. I began turning around, surveying my surroundings. When I was facing away from the apartment, off in the horizon between a few buildings, I could see the shadows of the pyramids. I exhaled, and whispered to Yasiin, "Is that what I think it is?"

"Just wait until the morning when you go sit on the balcony. You will be able to see it much better, my friend."

A sense of peace entered my body, meeting an excitement that I hadn't experienced before. It was that feeling of ènouement.

He picked up my bag and began carrying it up the ten wide steps leading into the building's entrance, which was large with double doors. We entered and climbed two flights of steps. At the landing of the first flight, he made sure to show me where Mohammed and his family lived. We got to the door of my apartment, and he began unlocking three different locks. When the apartment door opened, it was like I was transported back two or three decades into an enchanted place. I immediately noticed the gorgeous marble-like floor onto which I would eventually drop my iPhone and crack its screen. The apartment was dark, with dim lights shining from the gorgeously detailed brown light fixtures. There were multiple bedrooms, one and a half bathrooms, great textures on the walls, and furniture with carvings, patterned material, and lots of wood. I paid $210 for the ten days. *Not bad,* I thought, *as long as I don't die.*

The stove in the kitchen was a model I had never seen before. My grandmother might have seen one in the small town where she grew up in Alabama, because it was some antique-looking thing. Yasiin had already been by to turn on the air-conditioning units, so the apartment was cool. He also had water, juice, fruit, and freshly baked bread and hummus waiting for me.

After showing me how everything worked, he told me he would be back in the morning. "Lock the door, all locks. Open for nobody. I will introduce you to Mohammed and his family tomorrow."

As soon as I locked the door, I started sending my mom and friends voice notes, letting them know I was in an episode of the Showtime channel's show *Homeland.* At this point, the clock hit 2:45 a.m. I was exhausted, sweaty, tired, and on edge. I wanted a shower and sleep! I went into the full bathroom with the large, old, round standalone tub and turned on the shower... I waited and waited, but the water was only getting lukewarm. Not cold, not hot, lukewarm. I quickly got the point that a hot shower wasn't going to happen for the next ten days. Hot water was nothing I even thought to check for beforehand; I just took it for granted. In 100-degree heat, I guess most people don't need hot showers. Not having access to it, especially if they've never had it, is not a big deal to them. I took the quickest shower of my life, got ready for bed, and then locked the master bedroom door. After finally getting into the large bed, which had a decent mattress, my adrenaline was finally wearing off. I was left in pure silence. It felt like I was in a dream as I contemplated, *Is this real life? Am I actually in Egypt, alone? Not just Egypt, but in a real Egyptian home, from where I can see the pyramids?*

I'm guessing I finally fell asleep, lost in my thoughts, because no more than an hour or so later I hopped out of bed in fight mode. A loudspeaker and man's voice was occupying the whole space in an inescapable way. I didn't know if someone was in the apartment, if I was getting arrested, or what was going on... Then it hit me as I recognized the familiar sound; it was the call to the pre-dawn prayer, Fajr. A calm came over me and slowed down my speeding heart rate. I pulled back the silk curtains, and it was still as dark as night. I opened the window, letting the sound freely come in without the obstruction of the glass. I looked out the window and once again had an out-of-body moment that I can't describe in words. I thought to myself... *You are one crazy girl. You are in Giza, Egypt, in the midst of a chaotic time in the country, looking at the pyramids at a distance* (which look even more energetically powerful in the still of the night, just sitting there as a pillar of an ancient civilization that can't be destroyed, copied, or altered), *hearing the call to prayer, alone, the farthest you've ever been from home... ever.* A tear came down my face as the energy vortex of the land penetrated me.

I experienced that feeling of énouement once again — the bitter-sweetness of arriving in the future and not being able to tell your past self how it ends up. If only I could go back in time and give my former self a glimpse of what was to come, it would have made things so much easier. I vowed at that moment to never forget this feeling and to remember it every time I needed to trust the process and beauty of life. I crawled back into bed and went to sleep peacefully, full of energy, and smiling.

***

The sun beamed into the window as the sounds of the day were in full effect. Cars were honking, Arabic was spoken in different tones, and children were laughing. I jumped out of the bed as it dawned on me this would be my first time seeing Africa in the daylight. I looked out onto the sandy roads with trash neatly lining the street, and I noticed it looked even more like a place from another reality in the daytime. I smirked and then went to the refrigerator to get some fruit; I was starving.

With my fruit in hand, I decided to open the double doors onto the balcony; it was a straight line of sight to the pyramids! I stood on the balcony and tried to imagine what it was like when Hatshepsut, the second confirmed female pharaoh, was walking around this amazing land. She was a badass, reestablishing trade in the region as well as being one of the more amazing builders in both Upper and Lower Egypt. It was interesting to be looking out now, seeing all of the Arab influence first-hand. Most associate this with Egypt past and present. But I knew that in ancient times, this African land was filled with people who were closer to the color of rich, deep-colored oil rather than sand. At that moment I was contemplating whether I'd try and venture to Aswan alone, where the skin of the Nubian people was closer to the original inhabitants. I quickly reminded myself to be grateful for such a protective host, and that I should be more cautious than usual. Either way, I had already paid for the ten days here, so if I could find a way to go and return safely alone, I would take it.

Yasiin had left a local cell phone for me so we could communicate without me incurring any cell phone charges. *So thoughtful*, I said to myself. I called him and told him I wanted to see the pyramids up close as soon as possible. He laughed and was on his way.

***

As we turned the corner, the pyramids in all of their magnificence were on my left. A rush of emotion-inducing butterflies came over me as the structures got closer and closer, becoming less of a mirage. They were bigger and even more majestic in person.

"Wooooow," was all I could muster.

After passing through the entrance, I took my shoes off to actually feel the earth under my feet. When your feet connect with the ground, you're able to experience the energy of a place on another level. Energy rushed through my body, and I literally leaped in excitement.

Yasiin screamed, "Woooooaaaahhhh! Give me you phone, do again, I make picture."

Not knowing if I had another one in me, I looked at my surroundings, then leaped, getting pretty high off the ground. Thank goodness Yasiin captured the shot because there was no way that was happening again. A couple of men walked over and gave Yasiin a hug. He introduced me as Shosho, and the journey through one of the magical lands in Egypt I had dreamt of began.

I immediately noticed that there were hardly any visitors. Yasiin explained how tourism had plummeted at an alarming rate the past couple years. Everyone felt the hit financially.

We approached one of the pyramids, and the two men keeping watch greeted Yasiin warmly; I sensed they knew each other closely. He introduced me, and I received a warm greeting as well. I felt the ease of the energy between us all and knew this was a moment I'd never get back. I asked Yasiin if I could go down into the pyramid by myself while they caught up with one another, handing him my purse so they would know I didn't want to take any pictures and giving them less reasons to say no. Yasiin looked at the men. They nodded, giving me the okay.

"Be careful going down," Yasiin warned me as I began my descent. I wasn't waiting one second for someone to change their mind about me going alone, so I immediately started descending backwards on the incline, which had small ledges to set your feet on. It was like a tunnel. Holding on and taking each step slowly, I wanted to make sure I didn't slip or tumble. *Be careful. Be careful,* I kept telling myself.

When I approached the bottom, I felt a totally different energy. It was if something went through my body magnetically. I had heard about and studied the energy vortex at this location on the earth, but feeling it was an entirely different thing. These amazing ancient African minds were so advanced that the pyramids are located dead center of the landmass on earth and aligned in many different ways with the stars. It was advanced astronomy at its finest. It's no wonder the energy of the place is electrifying. I looked around and thought to myself, *You are inside a pyramid ALONE. A long way from the Carnegie Museum, kid.*

I took a few steps, looking around and exploring. It was mind-blowing knowing that this structure was thousands of years old and something that actual people had built. Not a myth or old wives' tale, but something you could tangibly experience and see the evidence of, clear as day. The weird energy kept pulsating through my body, which could have just been nerves but felt different. I closed my eyes and took it all in, staying in the present moment. Inhale. Exhale. When I finally opened my eyes, taking another look around, I saw a single hanging light that was illuminating the place. A sense of kenopsia came over me—the eerie atmosphere of an abandoned place mixed with that feeling you feel in an old basement or cave.

All of a sudden, my adventurous side started quickly dwindling. Seven minutes was enough. I got bugged out being alone in this ancient treasure I had dreamed of. Hauling my tail to the ladder like something was chasing me, I bolted up as if my life depended on it. Yasiin and the guards started laughing as they saw me hustling up.

"She run for her life!" the one man exclaimed.

Through his laughter, Yasiin asked, "Did you see your great-great-great-grandfather down there? Why you running?"

I looked at him with my eyes wide open. He continued laughing. I wasn't quite sure what I felt, but I definitely felt something. Even knowing of the energy vortex that was supposedly in the pyramids, experiencing it myself, and alone, was transcendent. I was in another realm of reality.

We bid adieu to the men, who I know were strategically placed there at that moment so I could have that experience I'll never forget. As Yasiin and I made our way around the rest of the grounds, he got more and more passionate, explaining everything to me. Vendors were all over the place, and because there weren't many tourists, to put it lightly, they were pretty aggressive. I'm not a fan of animal tourism at all. I look at it as another form of slavery. Riding a camel was absolutely out of the picture. I feel people's energy pretty strongly, and animals are no different. One particular vendor was pretty adamant in debating me about how I'd regret not taking a camel ride once I'd left. The particular camel he was trying to get me to ride was sad and angry, and I could feel it.

"I will not ride him, he is not happy and is quite sad," I told him.

"He is fine; he loves taking people around," the vendor replied.

Looking the poor camel in the eyes, I could feel his agony.

"Thanks but no thanks. Trust me, he is sad and angry."

When we turned to walk away, the camel started in a violent outburst, getting out of control. The vendor could barely control him as Yasiin grabbed me to make sure I got out of the way. I wanted to cry. The vendor ended up lashing him a few times as the camel fought for his freedom. I felt guilty, like I had provoked the poor little camel. It definitely put a damper on my time from that point.

A few moments later, Yasiin was having a lively lighthearted conversation with an attractive man in Arabic; I politely stood and waited for him to finish. The man kept intensely looking me in my eyes as I wondered what was being said. He finished up the conversation laughing, and we began walking.

Yasiin informed me what was supposedly said. "He ask how many camels to marry you, my cousin Shosho."

My eyes and face twisted, and I couldn't tell if he was joking or serious, so I laughed while blurting out, "What?!"

"No worry. I tell him no less than 100 camels because you beautiful and eyes very strong. Allah make you eyes like magic change colors. This will make it easy for husband to tell how to treat you at any moment based on you eye color," he said in such a way that I thought he might be serious.

I responded, "So what's the going rate for 100 camels? Will we be rich?" I was curious as to how much I was worth.

"Lots and lots and lots of money," he informed me, laughing at my humor.

We made our way over to where the great Sphinx was located, and I was in total amazement. A group of teenaged Saudi boys started talking to Yasiin, and he chuckled.

"They would like to take picture with you," he told me.

"With me? Ummm, okay," I agreed, smiling at the young men.

As they surrounded me, I felt like Mickey Mouse at Disney World. All I could do was laugh as they were all smiles with thumbs-up signs. I wondered what they would say when they showed the picture to their friends. I gave them a side-eye in my mind.

Once I laid my eyes on the Sphinx, I was in awe of its magnificence. Seeing how the nose was destroyed made it so much more real than the pictures. So many ancient Kemetic statues were defaced. I believe that this was to hide the African features of the native people of this land. Kemet literally translates to "the black land," although most people equate modern Egyptians with the Egyptians of the past, which is the equivalent of someone thinking the indigenous people of the United States look like today's Americans. The Arab conquest of and crusades into Egypt are the reason the country is home to a mostly Arab looking population, the same way the United States population looks the way it does because of the slaughter and conquest of Native Americans. Imagine a movie about Pocahontas where she is played by Cameron Diaz. That's exactly how I feel when I see ancient Egyptians played by people who are not indigenous African people.

After a few hours, in the beating heat, absorbing all I could absorb, my heart was content. I took one last look as we left and smiled on the inside.

***

I fell completely in love with the local food. Every day Yasiin brought me delicious food or took me to the local places I would never have found on my own. You know, the hidden spots in the nooks and crannies that the neighborhood people go to because they know the owner is an amazing cook. Anyone from the 'hood knows the local barbecue spot that's a hole-in-the-wall but has the best food in the city. I was eating in Giza's versions of these places every day.

I ate enough hummus and fresh bread to last me a year. The hummus was perfect; the taste was unlike anything I had ever experienced. It simply melted, the smooth texture complimented by a savory, rich flavor that exploded in my mouth with every bite.

The pita-like bread, *aish baladi*, was the perfect partner with all the Egyptian dishes. A staple in a typical Egyptian diet, seen as a key to nutrition, the name literally translates to "life."

Dating all the way back to ancient Egypt, wheat and barley have been heavily planted and used not only to bake but also as currency at times. Wheat was a sacred plant, and the baked goods made from it can be seen in some of the hieroglyphics. As I was eating the bread, I was aware I was also eating a piece of ancient history. "Breaking bread" with someone in Egypt is seen as one of the friendliest things you can do.

The beans were polished, with flavors new to my palette, and I loved every bite. I am a tea lover, and since tea is the national drink, I basked in every sip I was offered over and over again. The tea had an extremely strong taste that withstood even the heavy-handed sweetening.

Mohammed and his father, my guardians in the apartment building, came and checked on me a couple times a day, bringing me tea, snacks, and fruit. They spoke not a word of English, but somehow we communicated and got along quite well. Energy is my favorite language, so we had a good time trying to communicate with gestures and teaching each other words. I have to admit, I felt safer than I would have had they not been looking out for me.

I was able to witness a part of an Egyptian marriage celebration, go to local museums, and kick back and relax, reading on my balcony with the pyramids in the background. The call to prayer became so embedded in my subconscious that I grew fond of the loud sound that happened like clockwork. But nothing compared to the imam's recitation during jumu'ah, the Friday congregational prayer.

I had heard recitations many times, but this imam brought me to tears. I quickly hit record on my phone, sitting it in the window as I closed my eyes and listened to the loudspeaker from the local mosque that pushed every note of his chilling voice, which would forever become part of my DNA. You hear sounds that penetrate you to your core, and this was one of them. I was so grateful for the moment and thought about the likelihood that I would be in Giza alone, listening to the local imam through my window, watching the dirt road in front of me, and glimpsing the pyramids in the background at the same time. Wow. I was literally living in a story I couldn't have written myself.

I always ask the universe to arrange things beyond anything I can arrange myself, so I know it's beyond me. I try to never miss the signs, to follow the breadcrumbs, and to make a big deal out of even the smallest things. This was destiny… with so much evidence. I was in awe of the thread that connects the dots, no matter how tangled it may get. I do my part, and then let the magic happen. The thing is, I always expect the magic to happen!

***

My ten days had concluded, and my flight to Abu Dhabi was in the wee hours of the morning, around 3:00 a.m. Yasiin came to pick me up for the final time. He was excited to get me on my way. His anxiety could finally abate about the "cute" American girl he had to make sure left in one piece. He had just gotten into an accident a few hours before, leaving his daughter slightly injured, so when we got to the airport, I told him I'd be fine, that he could just drop me off. I promised to return, and he told me I must bring my brother or dad next time so I don't drive him crazy. We laughed.

It was midnight, dark, and this was unlike any airport entrance I had ever seen before. Absolute and extreme chaos is the only way I can describe it. There were herds and herds of people gathered outside, having a million different conversations in Arabic. There seemed to be no rhyme or reason to the aggressive clusters, and I didn't know what to do. No one I asked spoke English, and the doors into the airport were not open. It seemed as if everyone was just waiting outside. I had no clue how to get into the airport, and my flight was leaving in two hours and forty-five minutes. For the first time, I felt completely and extremely overwhelmed. I thought to myself, *You have exactly three minutes to freak out and have a meltdown, and then you must suck it up!*

I sent my mom a voice note, freaking out on my cracked phone, explaining how I might miss my flight because the airport seemed to be closed and nobody understood me. I was on the brink of tears when I overheard someone say that the doors would open at 12:30 a.m. It all made sense at that point, and I realized the clusters were lines into the airport. I saw a family with small children and decided to get in the line behind them. Right beside and behind me were some big men. Perfect, I thought. Nobody will push kids or these guys, so I should be good.

The clusters got bigger and bigger, and I got more anxious by the minute, just wanting to be on the plane out of there. The buzz of noise from the continuous conversations got louder and thicker. Finally, the doors opened. I realized we had to put our bags through a scanner and show our passports before entering the airport. The herds of people started pushing their way to the front of the line. It was a hot mess. I knew I had to put on my big girl panties and bring out my inner gangster to make sure I got in in a timely manner. I was pushed and shoved a bit, but I just kept edging my way forward. I finally made my way to the front as an older man started speaking to me in Arabic, asking for my passport. I suppose he was expecting Egyptian documents, because as I handed him my passport, his eyes widened as he looked around to see who I was with.

"Alone?!" he inquired, puzzled.

"Yes, sir," I responded.

He immediately grabbed my bag and put it through the scanner while saying something to a much younger man who took his post. Grabbing my arm, he simply said, "Come!" The next thing I knew, he grabbed my bag off the conveyer belt after it was scanned and escorted me to the front of the Etihad check-in counter, bypassing the line. He said a few things to the desk agent as he handed her my passport. She took my bag, tagged it, gave me my boarding pass and told me to have a good flight. My new self-appointed guardian guided me to the passport control line, smiled and said, "Safe travels. May Allah guide and protect you." I responded, "Thank you sooooo much, Alhamdulillah!" which translates to *praise be to Allah*. He smiled, seeing the deep appreciation in my eyes.

I took a minute in the line and reflected on the angels, Yasiin, Mohammed and his father, and now this elder, who had kept me safe and were my guides through my stay. My experience with Egyptian men was one of protection and kindness. I had made it in and out of Egypt safely alone while having an experience I will never forget. Next, I'd have a quick stay in Abu Dhabi, then it was off to see my best friend in Bahrain!

6

MAGIC CARPET

I wish I could buy me a spaceship and fly,
past the sky…

~Kanye West

Exhausted from the stress of solo traveling, I couldn't wait to see some familiar faces and spend a couple weeks with my best friend since the age of ten. Regina and her navy husband Cedric recently moved to Bahrain when he was stationed there. We'd had such a great time at their wedding in Hawaii—I couldn't wait to hang out with them again, since that was the last time we had seen each other. Cedric was like the big brother I never had. The running joke in Hawaii was him ordering me kiddie juice boxes at every restaurant we went to because I've never had alcohol. When the two of us get together, it's intellectual debates and rip sessions for days. Regina just laughs and says she married the male version of me. She and I are each other's biggest cheerleaders, and her mother called me her pit bull, telling everyone in Hawaii, "You better not let Shawna hear you say anything remotely bad about Regina, or she will come for you! No questions asked."

She is my person. When people ask what that is, we always repeat the line from *Grey's Anatomy* when Christina Yang explained her relationship with Meredith Grey: "If I killed someone, she's the person I'd call to help me drag the body across the floor and bury it." We always add, "And she wouldn't ask me what happened until the body was deep into the ground." Disclaimer: obviously we wouldn't really kill anyone, but it's a loyalty and love that runs deep and has formed over two and a half decades.

I finally arrived, but as I was going through passport control, the officer asked me to have a seat. Baffled by what was going on, I waited exactly where I was told. After taking my passport from me, he entered a room with a much meaner-looking man.

They were going back and forth, inspecting my passport, and I had no clue what the problem or hold-up was. Upon his return, he asked me a series of questions. I stayed incredibly calm and answered politely.

"Why have you been to all these places in the last month?" he questioned.

"I'm taking a trip around the world," I answered, amused at how it sounded out loud.

"By yourself?" His voice rose an octave as he looked at me strangely.

"Yes sir. Just me," I said, returning his eye contact.

"Why are you staying in Bahrain for two weeks?" he interrogated.

"My best friend's husband is stationed here in the US Navy. I am coming to visit them," I informed him.

That must have satisfied his curiosity. He looked me in the eyes for five seconds as if he was still trying to figure me out, then approved me to enter the country.

"Enjoy your visit, and be safe, adventure girl," he said, shaking his head as he smiled.

When I finally saw Regina's face, I just sighed in relief.

"Oh my God, I can't believe you're really here!" she screamed at the top of her lungs while welcoming me into her arms.

"I've never been so happy to see you in my life!" I uttered in relief, meaning every single word. I was exhausted from navigating the world alone.

When we got to their amazing apartment, I was so happy to have hot water, halfway reliable but slow internet, central air, and modern amenities. Plus, I knew I was safe for the next couple of weeks, which allowed me to come off my extended rush. Sleeping for twenty-four hours was not the plan, but somehow, my first day, I couldn't move and didn't want to.

The next day we headed to the market, where the sounds of hustle and bustle drowned out my thoughts as we made our way through. I was invigorated by all the excitement—getting a piece of fruit was an adventure in itself. The one thing that threw me off was the number of immigrants from Pakistan, Bangladesh, and other countries, performing menial labor. I found out after a few conversations that some of these men had earned engineering degrees in their home countries but could make more money here as service workers and then send money back home. I could see the difference in how they were treated. I didn't like it.

Over the next two weeks, I had such an amazing time, eating at the many amazing Bahraini restaurants, going to the bustling markets and the local souk, bartering prices for oils and things. I had dinner at new friends' houses, went to lounges, and even attended the navy ball, where I got invited to the marines ball, but I was leaving before it would take place. I had the best pancakes I've ever had in my life in Bahrain, and I would go back just to get another taste.

***

My time in Northern Africa and the Middle East had been amazing but was coming to an end. There was just one thing I deeply regretted not doing in Egypt or Abu Dhabi: riding an ATV in the desert. Riding the ATVs in Hawaii gave me such an adrenaline rush. I couldn't believe I hadn't managed it. I searched and couldn't find a place to rent ATVs in the deserts of Bahrain, so I figured it was just not going to happen, but I secretly hoped somehow it would. On our way to Bahrain's little desert, I told Regina my one wish. All of a sudden, not even moments after the words left my mouth, dust was kicking up left and right, instigated by a swarm of Bahraini men on dirt bikes and ATVs.

"No freaking way!" I announced, not believing what I was seeing. "I have to find them so I can ride! It's a sign; I just said I wanted to ride ATVs!" I continued.

It looked as if they were leaving. We, on the other hand, were just getting there, but I knew the universe wouldn't tease me like that. That would just be cruel. Regina and I parked and proceeded to walk around the desert. The ATVs seemed to be long gone, and I was hot after an hour in the sand. As we were heading back to the car, the biker gang with their loud exhaust and motors came storming back, zipping past us. Not being one to let a moment pass me by twice, I start excitedly waving them down, running towards them as if I knew them. The leader stalled and stopped to see what the heck we wanted. I had second thoughts for half a second but snapped out of it when I heard Regina screaming, "Can my friend ride? She's here all the way from America!"

He gave me the 'hell yeah' face, putting his arms up while saying, "Come on! Let's go!"

I handed Regina the few items I had, hiked up my long dress, and hopped on the back of his ATV.

He screamed, "Hold on!" over the blazing sound of his motor, and so I did.

Slightly shocked when I realized he was drenched in sweat from riding for hours in this desert heat, the next thing I knew, we were speeding across the sand. He was maneuvering the ATV like it was something he'd done a thousand times before. When he started popping wheelies, my adrenaline kicked all the way in. One of my favorite things in the world is a great rollercoaster, so this was right up my alley. The authenticity of my screams and laughs made him really start showing off. *This is way better than riding an ATV alone – this is next level!*

The sun began making its descent, slowly disappearing into the horizon, and we looked like something out of the Arabian Nights. My heart was racing as fast as a jaguar can run, and the sand kicked up at every turn we made. There were a couple times I was sure we were going to tip back, and I'd fall off, but I had gotten accustomed to the thrill. I was screaming, the sound of pure, unadulterated freedom. I felt exhilarated.

Ask and it is given. I asked, and ended up with the ATV ride of a lifetime. Finally, as we headed back to where Regina and the rest of his crew were waiting, the ATV got caught in the sand. My adrenaline was so high at that point that when we hopped off, I lifted the back of the ATV up as if I were a Dora Milaje warrior while he was maneuvering it out in the front. He looked at me with a "what in the world?" face and started laughing.

Regina walked over, more excited than I was, screaming, "Yooooo, did you really just lift that? You're crazy! How cool was that ride?! Oh my God!"

"Man that was so much fun… I can't believe this just happened!" I spilled, not being able to contain my excitement.

I had a brief exchange with the young man, who was super cool and let me know we could go out on jet skis next if I wanted. He promised it would be just as much fun. The last time I had been on a jet ski, I think I scraped some skin off my dad's chest from holding on so tight as he dare-deviled his way through the water. I was leaving the next day, but I promised next time I was in the area, I'd return for part two. I could only imagine how crazy he would be on a jet ski. I took some pictures with the guys, and my heart was completely content. The fact I had manifested something out of thin air may have tickled me more than the actual ride, although the ride was beyond amazing.

The sun was starting to fall quickly at that point, so we knew it was time to head back into the city. The guys rode off into the distance while Regina began to drive back toward the road. As we were driving through the sand, all of a sudden, the car wouldn't move. At all. It was almost like we were stuck in a pile of snow, which we are used to, being we are both from snowy Pittsburgh originally. This was different, and worse! The more she tried to manipulate the car and push on the gas... the more the front tires dug into the sand.

"We are really stuck. I don't know what to do." Regina panicked.

"We have to call Cedric to come get us, but we will never hear the end of it, man..." I said, knowing if Cedric came all the way out there to get us, it was going to be jokes for days after he questioned why we drove through the obvious deep part of the sand.

The one thing we knew was that we didn't want to get stuck out there in the dark. Right when we were about to make the dreaded call, a truck full of Bahraini men pulled up. They told us to get out of the car, and they started digging the sand out from around the wheels. It wasn't working. Nothing was working! They had a rope in their SUV and attached it to the back of our car and the back of their truck.

Attempt number one... They started driving the truck, thinking it would pull the car out, but the rope just snapped. The car was still in the sand. They dug more sand out from around the wheels by hand for seven more minutes and secured the rope tighter. Attempt number two... No luck. They attempted once again, and as the saying goes, the third time's a charm. The car backed out with ease, and one of the men drove it to an area where we could take over without getting stuck again.

We were so thankful and relieved that you would have thought we'd just won the lottery. Regina screamed, "Thank you!"

"Thank you! Thank you! Thank you! Alhamdulillah!" I exclaimed to the man who drove the car and got it out.

Finally, we were leaving the desert after my wish had been granted and another adventure completed. *Masha'Allah,* meaning God has willed it. I was leaving the next day and thought about how when I ask for something without a fear and attachment, the Universe drops it into my lap. I simply had a thought of how I really wanted to ride ATVs, then God thought he'd show off by not only giving me a better experience than I would have had riding one on my own, but I didn't even have to pay for it. It appeared like a magic carpet and came complete with an attractive Aladdin attached!

I hear the whispers and I see the winks of my ancestors as the smallest coincidences make me like a giddy school girl in celebration. I surrender to the red string of fate that is woven in my life in a magical way. I believe the universe is always conspiring in my favor, and I look for the evidence to support my theory. As *A Course in Miracles* states, "Miracles are natural, and when they do not occur something has gone wrong." One day, every second of every day will feel like magic. I am getting closer by the minute.

7

WHO LET THE DOGS OUT?

…Woof, woof, woof, woof, woof!

~Baha Men

Landing in Chiang Mai, Thailand, a sense of calm rushed over my mind and body. I had just sprinted through Paris, Egypt, Abu Dhabi, and Bahrain in the span of a month and some change. Now I'd have three to four weeks to experience Thailand before possibly heading to Bali. I hadn't bought a ticket out of the country yet; I had decided to just go with the flow and see what happened in Thailand. I had a hunch.

When I exited the airport, I grabbed a taxi. The driver, a short, thin but obviously toned, middle-aged Thai man placed my bags in the trunk. He greeted me with the warmest smile, and I immediately understood why Thailand is called "the Land of Smiles." I felt safe. I felt warm. I felt at peace. I had booked a studio on Airbnb in a 98% Thai neighborhood, where I would soon find out nobody spoke English. Although there were very few foreigners in the neighborhood, the man who owned the building was Korean American, married to a lovely Thai woman. As soon as I got out of the taxi, he was waiting for me outside. We had a ten-minute chat, and he told me where to eat and wash my clothes, what to look out for, and the low-down on where to get my drinking water, which he provided. Little did I know at the time, this conversation with my host would be the extent of my English interactions for a while.

My room was on the third of three floors, and as I passed the other studio apartments, I immediately noticed the shoes lined up outside the doors. Even though I arrived pretty early in the day, my body didn't forget it had just crossed time zones and endured another long flight. I wanted to do two things: shower and eat! The room was minimally but tastefully furnished with lots of open space, and it was extremely clean. In the front of the apartment building, I could see Doi Suthep Mountain in the distance through the huge window that let in an ample amount of light. The studio had a small kitchenette area that was perfect to refrigerate or heat up food and make rice or tea. I set my bags down, then immediately headed for the bathroom.

I was a bit perplexed when I entered and couldn't find a shower or tub. *Ummmmmmmmm...?* wondered my privileged western mind. The bathroom was big, had newer fixtures, nice tiling and floors, but it was just the toilet and sink on one side with a modern mirror and shelving. On the opposite wall was a box the size of a shoebox. I soon figured out the shoebox-sized thing was the water heater, because it had a hand-held shower-head.

"What in the fresh hell is this?" I actually blurted out.

After investigating, I realized there was a drain on floor. The entire floor was tiled, so I concluded the entire bathroom *was* the shower.

One of my biggest pet peeves is a wet bathroom floor. So much so, I had a separate bathroom from Kamau for most of the years we lived together, because he wouldn't dry his feet when he got out of the shower. I had to laugh, thinking how he would find it funny I couldn't escape a wet floor for at least the next ten days. I had to come up with a plan, or else I was going to lose my mind. I figured out that if I carefully showered in the one corner, being super diligent in where I aimed the shower hose, I could keep the rest of the bathroom from getting wet. Winning! I also used the extra towel I was given to dry the floor after showering. I'm one of those weird people who brushes her teeth in the shower, but that would not be happening—I'd be using the sink for sure!

After my shower adventure and getting my things settled in, I had one target—FOOD! I put on a colorful sundress to match my mood, slung my purse around me like a messenger bag to keep it secure, grabbed my selfie stick (moreso in case I needed a weapon), and opened the door to leave for my day one adventure.

I had no clue which way to go, but I saw an alley a few blocks down that seemed to have lots of people turning into it. I was in a residential neighborhood, so there wasn't a lot of activity when I opened the gate and exited the apartment driveway on foot. I got about half a block down the street when a spool of school-aged kids around seven years old saw and met me with an excitement and curiosity I had not witnessed before. They surrounded me, smiling, laughing, and talking in Thai, to which I could only make out one word, "Sawasdeeekhhaaaaaa!" (Hello).

The one thing I was absolutely sure of was that they were mesmerized with my long, wild, and wavy hair that I had secured with only a headband to keep it off my face. I told them in English it was okay to touch it and motioned for them to go ahead. Some sounds are universal, so I knew the "ahhhhhhhs" and "ohhhhhhhs" mixed with laughs and smiles meant they were happy with their findings. I can only imagine what they went home and told their parents. "Mom, today we saw a weird-looking girl, same color as us but different face and big, big hair. She let us touch her hair, and it was sooo big!" I still laugh thinking about it.

After our three-minute encounter, we went our separate ways, and I quickly remembered how hungry I was. I was almost to the alley that I had decided would be my best bet for food, when I saw three huge dogs, just chilling. No leash, no human companion nearby, just them looking at me and wondering what the heck I was doing, because they sensed I obviously didn't belong. I stopped, stayed calm, and watched them back, trying to gauge if I was going to have to use my selfie stick. There was no way I could get to the alley without walking past them. I could clearly see there were tons of people in the alley, so the dogs couldn't be *that* dangerous, right? My adrenaline kicked in, and I grabbed my selfie stick tight. I love animals, but if those fools attacked me, I was going down with a fight if my dog whisperer skills didn't work.

I began to walk towards them. All three rose to attention, watching my every move as I approached the alley and made the turn. Little did I know, their attention on me would be increased times ten the moment I turned down the alley and was met by thirty pairs of Thai eyes that stopped doing various things to see the specimen that had just entered their world. I blurted out "Woah!" instinctually and chuckled as I walked. There were four old men playing Makruk, which I would later find out is Thai chess; they stopped their game while dropping their jaws. One was saying something to me with a big smile on his face. I smiled back saying, "Sawasdeeeekhaaa," having not a clue what he'd said. I kept walking, trying to "act like I belonged," which is my traveling motto. If you act like you're supposed to be there, people will think you're supposed to be there. The only thing is, I stuck out like that one grey hair that always seems to find its way on your hairline no matter how many times you pluck it out.

I was parting the Red Sea as I walked, and everyone moved out of my way, staring in amazement. And I mean... *really staring*. I noticed about six more huge dogs as I walked the three blocks to the end of the street, and I quickly realized big dogs are like random cats in the United States. I didn't stop at any of the small food tables that were set up and didn't really get a good lay of the land. Somehow I had forgotten how hungry I was in that five minutes and was just trying to make it through. Feeling a sense of relief when I got to the end of the street, I saw a small restaurant that was an actual restaurant. I decided to cross the road to check it out. I was quickly reminded that the traffic moves the opposite direction than back home, because as I was looking to the left, the cars were zooming by from my right. Small things like that always reminded me that, like Dorothy in *The Wizard of Oz*, I wasn't in Kansas anymore, and Toto was the 200-pound dog watching me from across the street.

I finally made my way across after zipping and zagging through the passing motorbikes with entire families—and I mean five people—on them. I was amazed at how a dad, mom, baby, toddler, and older sibling were all on one motorbike with bags *and* drinks in hand. Every neck in a car, truck, and motorbike that passed by me strained to look at me. It was as if I were a unicorn, alien, or Michael Jackson awakened from the dead. I finally entered the restaurant, and the smell of ginger and lemongrass immediately woke up my senses. An older, round, yet somehow still lean and strong woman approached me, smiling with kind eyes that met my chin. She looked up at me, touched my face, and said something I couldn't make out. Her voice and smile let me know I was in good hands. I smiled, laughed, and grabbed her extended hand as she led me to sit down. Looking at the menu, I realized that not only could I not understand a word but not even a letter. The numbers were the only things familiar. I'm vegan now (that story comes later), but at that time, I hadn't eaten pork or beef in twenty years, since I was thirteen. So I did the only thing I knew would get the message across—I started acting out a chicken and making chicken sounds. Here I am in a Thai restaurant, at the table, making chicken noises and flapping my arms. This excited the child I guessed to be the older woman's seven-year-old granddaughter, who was seated behind the counter, cracking up at my attempt at ordering chicken.

The woman let out a chuckle and let out an "ahhhhhhh," letting me know she understood, then carried on in Thai as she made a drinking motion.

I said, "Coconut," praying she'd understand that word—which she did.

"Yes. Coconut," she repeated as she collected the menu and walked away.

At that moment, I looked around and realized I was in freaking Thailand and had another out-of-body experience. This was not a test.

Ten minutes later, my new auntie brought me a cup of cold coconut juice and a huge plate of chicken Pad Thai. The first bite made it obvious that I had not had authentic Pad Thai before I was today years old. Whatever Thai food I had eaten in the States was a shadow of what I was feasting on in that moment. I devoured every single bite. But as soon as I was done with my food, the older woman set something that looked like mango and rice in front of me, gesturing for me to eat it. I hesitated, then cut through the mango, getting some of the rice and crazy cream-like mixture on my spoon as well. As I raised the spoon up to my mouth, the sweet scent entered my nose before I put it in my mouth. I was tasting mango sticky rice for the first time. I have a sweet tooth, and this was a pure succulent piece of heaven. I couldn't resist — a "Mmmmmmmm" naturally purred from my lips as all the flavors mixed on my tongue — to the woman's amusement. She leaned back, clapped, and laughed all at once.

As I was eating, she dropped off the bill that read 83 baht. I wasn't up on the conversion rate yet, being I had just been in Bahrain and using an entirely different currency for a couple weeks, so I pulled out my money conversion app. Thinking the number must have been a mistake, I looked all over the bill to find the rest of the numbers. 83 baht was the total cost, which is around $2.50. That's around the same price of the food in Egypt. I thought, *I may never leave here!* as I laid down 120 baht, cause I'm balling like that! I got up and turned towards the woman. I drew my hands together in front of my chest and bowed; it is called the *wai*. She smiled, saying, "You back," making sure I knew to return.

Feeling full and satisfied, I skipped out of the restaurant in a peaceful mood. Oh my goodness, it was already dark at only 6:00 p.m.! This meant I had to go through the lion's den of dogs in the dark to get back home. I crossed the street and approached the alley, noticing about seventy percent fewer people but *more* dogs. All the food vendors and small shop-owners were closing up and breaking their tables down. I took a deep breath, put one earphone bud in, and turned on JayZ's song, "What More Can I Say?" If anything could get me through this moment, it was my alter-ego JayZ... so I began walking down the alley.

The dogs, watching every single step I took, were slightly more intrigued than the last time. The alley looked completely different and scarier in the dark, so I was on 100% alert. I had one mission—make it through the alley alive! Dramatic, I know, but all I could imagine was my mom's face if she got a call from the US Embassy letting her know I had been eaten alive by a pack of stray dogs. She would stop her hysterical crying and laugh for half a second when they told her JayZ was playing in my headphones when they found me. She would know at least I went out with Shawn Carter in my ears before she'd return to her hysterical crying. I'm normally not afraid of dogs at all, but when you have eight huge dogs looking your way, you realize there is at least a ten percent chance you're in danger. I had laser focus — get to the end of the alley. I started walking at a fast pace, and before I knew it, I could finally see the old men still playing Makruk at the corner table. At that point, I knew I would most likely make it out alive. When I turned the corner and saw my apartment building a block away, I was relieved. Little did I know, my animal adventures were just beginning.

I walked up the three flights of steps leading to my place, slipped out of my shoes at the door, put my key in the lock, opened the door, and turned on the light. I immediately saw a tiny green lizard-like thing, the size of my pinky, dashing into the room from outside and up the wall. I took a deep breath and held in what my normal reaction would be, which is panic. It was similar to the little lizards I had seen in Puerto Rico and Phoenix, but this thing was now in my house! To put this in context, I moved out of a downtown Philadelphia apartment that I loved because I saw a mouse there. Living with fast-moving things that I didn't invite in was not my idea of okay. I immediately went to the internet and looked up "Little Lizards in Thailand," discovering it was a common house gecko and considered good luck. Ummmm, you're not in Kansas anymore, Dorothy, and now Toto is not a dog but a gecko.

I was involuntarily forced out of my comfort zone once again, because there was nobody to call, nowhere to go, and I was on my own. I decided to suck it up and put my big girl pants on, since everything I read said that they were harmless. I realized it was only 6:00 a.m. back home in the States, so nobody would be awake. It hit me, I'm in freaking Thailand — the farthest away I could ever be on the planet from Pittsburgh, PA — and alone!

I looked my fear in the eyes, sat with it, logically thought it through, and moved on. I call fear my overprotective big brother that only wants to protect me. He gets some of his information from instincts, but some is just him being overprotective. In this case, based on my previous experiences with mice, he was just trying to keep me safe. But, after thinking it through, I was forced to tell him that the information he had gotten was false, and I'd be okay, little lizard and all.

I laughed out loud, then decided I was exhausted. I fell asleep after contemplating for an hour what the little lizard might be doing.

***

Over the next ten days, I felt the most isolation I think I've ever experienced in my life. I welcomed it. I couldn't run from my thoughts, and there was nobody to rely on. Nobody to talk to. No chatter from the outside world because I couldn't understand a word anyone around me was saying. I realized I was exhausted mentally, spiritually, physically, and emotionally. The solitude was solitude, not to be confused with loneliness. It was eye-opening.

I needed the isolation. I needed the space where *only I* existed. I needed to explore, witness, love on, release, and reprogram my unconscious thoughts. I needed to lie in bed all day or do nothing without anyone expecting, wanting, or needing anything from me. I had nobody to answer to, and there was nowhere to be except exactly where I was.

I made my way down the alley a couple times a day; by now everyone was used to seeing my face and waved, or at least didn't stare as much. Different shop owners would call me over to try this and that. I was like the neighborhood pet, replacing the large dogs who always lurked around. After about five days, the dogs and I became friendly; I was petting and feeding them daily. I ate at my restaurant at least once a day, and the older woman was just as excited as the day before every time I walked in. In the alley was another older woman who made the best Thai iced tea at a simple table outside her house. Stopping by to see her in the morning and evening became a ritual. The tea was thirty cents. She taught me a new word upon every meeting, and I realized quickly that Thai was a language that would be challenging to absorb.

I was twelve hours ahead of the States, living in the future, so I didn't have much interaction with my friends and family back home. Text and phone tag became the norm. I decided once my ten days in this apartment was up, I was going to move to a different section of the city where there might be a chance for me to speak English, if only a couple words a day. Little did I know, that decision would lead to my full Thai immersion.

8

YOU'VE GOT TO HAVE FAITH

Be grateful for blessings. Don't ever change,
keep your essence.

~Tupac

I packed up my belongings into my single suitcase and backpack and moved to my new place in Old City. There were tons of people—Thai people, Chinese people, white people... A sigh of relief came over me when I even saw few words in English!

I still had not seen another black person, and I figured at that point it just wasn't going to happen. On my way home one evening, walking down a side street, I saw beautifully rich dark brown skin with short locs framing the glowing face of what I thought was a mirage. It was a gorgeous black girl! Not being able to contain my excitement, I smiled the biggest smile I think I've ever let out and automatically raised my arms.

She matched my enthusiasm as we blurted out "Hellloooo!" at the same time.

"Where are you from? I'm Faith!" she said with an accent I couldn't quite make out.

"I'm from the United States; I'm Shawna. I'm soooo happy to see you. I was starting to think I was never going to see a black person again!" I joked, to which she cracked up, nodding her head to let me know she shared the sentiment.

We decided we weren't going to let the moment pass us by; we found the nearest café and grabbed dinner. You would have thought we'd known each other for years the way we were laughing for hours. In the midst of one of our chattering and laughing fits, a big Australian man around sixty-five years young, who looked like he'd ridden every type of motorcycle known to man and was sitting at a table near us interrupted, laughing. "You ladies are having a blast! How long have you been in Thailand?" he inquired with his thick accent.

"We actually just met two hours ago. But I've been here a few weeks," I said while Faith smiled, waiting for his reaction.

"No way! You guys are carrying on like old mates," he said, confused but curious and tickled.

I would call that man Uncle Jack every time I ran into him, my white Australian uncle. Every time I saw him, I'd scream, "Uncle Jack!" and people would look so confused.

I learned Faith was from rural Zimbabwe but moved to the UK in her late teens. She had been all over Africa and Europe and now was making her way through Asia for the next couple of months. Her energy was electrifying, and I told her a million times she has to write a book. I was mesmerized hearing about her life as a child in the countryside of Zimbabwe. Stories of her father, family, food, and schooling experiences were like watching a movie I never wanted to end. Equally intriguing was her adjustment to life in the UK. She, in turn, loved learning about the past and modern struggles of black folks in the States and was happy to hear a firsthand account of what was actually going on with the killing of so many young black men by the police that was all over the news. We decided to link back up during the next couple days before she jetted off to her next destination. We went to the markets, found a great pizza spot, and had a good ole time. She left after a few days, and I was back to me, myself, and I. Or so I thought.

I had a voice note from my friend, Tajiddin. I was excited to chat with him, because the time difference made it hard to have a conversation with anyone back home. Our relationship is like oil and water. Within ten minutes of any conversation, it doesn't matter the topic, we are in a deep intellectual or philosophical debate. Sometimes we are saying the exact same thing, but somehow, one of us becomes the devil's advocate. Mental gymnastics. Ironically, we've remained friends for eight-plus years, and after our debates, we always resume regular conversation like we weren't just about to kill one another. I think we were brother and sister in a former life; that's the only explanation.

That day's mental match was how nothing on earth could make me date anyone but a black man.

We'd had this conversation a few years before while walking down the street in Harlem, NY, when an older man walking nearby interjected himself into the conversation because he found it so interesting. This was an ongoing debate.

"Dude, I'm only attracted to black men. I love black men. There is a zero percent chance I would ever date anyone but a black man. I'm friends with men of other races, but it won't ever happen!" I pronounced.

"I see what you're saying and have no problem with your preference. Keyword preference. My problem is the absolute. You don't know what is going to happen! And you're telling me if you met a man randomly whom you really liked and then became attracted to, you wouldn't date him because he's not black? Get the heck out of here, that's the dumbest thing I've heard you say! You're smarter than that."

"What I'm saying is, there's no way I'd be attracted to a man who's not black... YES, ABSOLUTE statement!"

9

RED PILL

You that red pill a (chick) found in the Matrix…

~J. Cole

The next day while I was out and about, I had an intense craving for fruit. Lots of fruit. I was craving mangos, pineapples, and whatever else I could sink my teeth into. I hopped over to a street I knew had lots of local vendors and started searching for the perfect mangos.

Suddenly, I heard a deep, raspy voice with a weird accent behind me, "Hello! Hola!"

I turned around to find an Asian man with skin kissed by the sun just enough to make his beautiful, full lips a hint of brown. His long silky hair dangled perfectly, draping his deep Asian eyes, high cheek bones, broad shoulders, and muscular arms, down to his waist. *Damn,* is all I thought, *this is one gorgeous human being.*

I replied, "Hello," but before I could say anything else he had the ends of my hair in between his fingers.

"You amazing. Wow. So pretty. What you look for?" he said, simultaneously smiling and glancing between his fingers full of my hair and looking me dead in the eyes.

"Fruit," I answered while brushing his hand out of my hair and twisting my face.

He immediately grabbed my hand, pulling me, while his deep voice echoed through his heavy accent, "I will take you to best fruit. Come."

We were walking when I realized we were going to his motorbike because he was now straddling it. The engine roared as he commanded me to hop on the back by smacking the seat behind him. I've been riding motorcycles all my life... My stepdad put me on the back of his Ninja motorcycle at age seven, but, ummm, I was in Thailand, and this was a stranger. At that moment, I noticed he was not built like your typical Thai man. He had some bulk to him with an interesting tattoo adorning his bicep.

Not bad, not bad at all, I thought before being snapped out of my admiration by his accent, gorgeous smile, and deep honest eyes. "You safe, you safe with me, I good guy! You want fruit, no?"

I pulled my skirt up and whipped my leg across the bike, thinking *YOLO* (you only live once). He grabbed my hands and put them around his waist, telling me to hold on. His hair immediately flew into my face, smelling refreshingly clean as the wind caught it with his acceleration. We came to a stoplight, and he leaned back to ask me if I was all right.

"Slow down," was all I said, to which he just laughed, telling me, "I'm going as slow as I can! No more slower."

Five minutes later, we arrived at a random corner with a family selling loads and loads of all the fruit you can imagine. It was fruit heaven! He hopped off the bike, then extended his hand to help me off as he blurted out "Pa!" which translates to an informal "come" or "let's go." As I followed behind him, I realized his back was pretty muscular. He lifted the back of his shirt to straighten it, and I could see along with being muscular his back was also covered in tattoos. I couldn't get a good look at the tattoo in its entirety, but I could clearly see he walked like he owned the entire world: cool, confident, deliberate, but full of life. An older woman and man watched us approaching and greeted him with huge smiles, patting him on the back. He and the older man had a brief exchange of words. The man and woman both looked at me joyfully, saying something I couldn't understand. Thai Man, which is what we will call this crazy gorgeous man whose bike I had just ridden, interpreted their exchange, telling me they said I was beautiful and have eyes like a rare tiger. Letting out my signature nervous laugh when receiving unexpected compliments, I bowed while singing the phrase, "Khob Khun ka" or thank you. The lady grabbed some random pieces of fruit that looked as juicy and colorful as a perfect sunset on a clear day, putting them in a plastic bag and handing them to

Thai Man. In return, he handed her some baht while looking at me, smiling and saying, "Pa."

I asked him how much I owed him, to which he whined out, "No problem, no problem," obviously annoyed that I'd think he wanted my money for the assortment of fruit he secured for 55 baht, which is around 1.50 USD.

"Where next?" he asked.

"You can take me back where you dropped me off," I replied.

"Then you go where?" he questioned.

"Home."

"So I just take you home. Where?"

I hesitated for ten seconds as he intently looked me in the eyes, never breaking his gaze. I was acting completely out of character. I'd just met this guy fifteen minutes before, but... I gave him the address.

Once again I was on the back of his bike, pulling up to my building seven minutes later. Ready to say goodbye forever, I thanked him for the fruit when he informed me I needed to be ready at 7:00 p.m., because he was coming back to pick me up. We were going to a concert and carnival. I knew it wasn't a request, even though he had a smile on his face the entire time.

I'm extremely assertive, and I love Alpha males, but this was just hilarious. I thought to myself, *I'm getting handled by a random Thai man. What is going on?*

I stood silently with a perplexed look on my face, about to put up a fight when he interrupted my thoughts once again. "You not do anything, anyway—come on. We have fun. I like you, you good energy, you pretty, you smell good." He paused, "See you seven, okay?"

I sighed and said, "Okay," partially because he spoke good English, and I was yearning for some more communication.

6:50 p.m.

My hair was in a high knot, tight black jeans hugged my legs, a black ruffled tank top clung to my body, and huge hoop earrings dangled from my ears. Waiting downstairs in the open-air entrance of my new place, I heard something that sounded like a sports car shifting gears as it came down the street, which was usually pretty quiet by this time of night. Suddenly I saw nothing but red. I said in sarcastic disbelief under my breath, "You have got to be kidding me." I felt like I was in a bad parody, because this car fit every car stereotype available for young Asian American men, in California especially, who pimp out their cars. All I could think of was my Korean American friend Jake back in Philly. We were into the same kind of indie movies, and on our movie outings, he would pick me up in his tricked out BMW. Thai Man's bright red car had to have about twenty-five different things that he'd switched out to customize it, and of course it was a Honda, stick shift, with tinted windows. I'd later find out this was his good car! He had a beat-up one he drove around in the mountains, to carry things around, and for his business.

He pulled up and got out smiling, but before getting in, there were a couple things I had to do. I walked to the back and took a picture of his license plate. His eyes were fixed on my every move, trying to figure out what I was doing. He was also obviously admiring my frame, and his face showed it. I took a picture of him next, as he looked even more baffled. I sent a text with these two attachments to my best friend Regina, telling her if she didn't hear from me in three hours to send it to my dad and tell him to come get me. I also sent one to my Aussie friend Mylinda I'd met in Paris; if I went missing they'd know who to track down. Thai Man asked me what the heck I was doing, so I looked him in the eyes and told him straight.

Thinking it was hilarious, he confidently asserted, "I protect you. I no hurt you, silly girl!"

In Thailand, the driver sits on the right side, which I never got used to, so I accidentally walked over to the driver's side. He laughed, asking me if I was driving. Then he told me, "Other side," and he opened my door. I finally got into the car on the correct side and shook my head when I noticed the inside of the car had customized lights on the floor.

"Let me guess, *Fast and Furious* is one of your favorite movies?" I teased once he was in the driver's seat.

"*Fast and Furious* is one of BEST movies!" he exclaimed.

"I was joking..."

"No joking. Good movie! I see all."

We drove off after I made sure my seat belt was secured, thinking I might be in for a crazy ride with this crazy man. My senses were heightened as I realized he was wearing an oil that mixed with his body chemistry extremely well. Not just any oil, the best-smelling oil my nose had ever encountered, and I'm an oil girl. In fact, I had just stocked up on ten bottles of exotic oils in Bahrain before coming to Thailand. I closed my eyes and took in the fragrance. It was woody, earthy, and sweet at the same time, but not even a slight bit overpowering, as oils often are. It smelled absolutely divine, and at that moment, I realized I didn't know exactly where we were going, but for some reason, I felt safe. He had pure energy, childlike, but extremely masculine. It was a weird combination I'd never encountered and was quite intrigued by.

I suppose he was equally as intrigued by me, because my thoughts were interrupted by his accented voice. "I never see hair and skin and eyes and lips like you on one person—why you look like that?"

I laughed and said, "I guess my mom and dad made a weird mix of a human. I'm just a black girl from America."

"Noooo, you not bwack." He couldn't pronounce black with an L. "You skin lighter me," he proclaimed as the rasp in his voice accompanied a growl.

"I'm definitely black. I'm black. No Asian, no white, just black."

"No girls anywhere look like you. And I been to Europe and Congo in Africa. Nowhere I see you face."

"There are many, many girls who look like me, especially in America. I haven't seen many Thai men who look like you!" I hit back immediately.

"I Thai. I grow up poor in mountains. But my dad Chinese and my mom half Indian. I grow up, then was monk. I want to live my life, so stop being monk and move to Europe ten years. Myself learn English, Portuguese, Spanish, French. Move back here three years."

Hearing that he was technically Chinese, Indian, and Thai helped me make sense of his appearance.

"You taught yourself all the languages?" Now I was super intrigued.

"Yes. Buy book and teach. Twenty-one learn English."

"You were a monk?"

Wait a minute, I'm in the car with a tatted up, long-haired former monk who's been to the Congo, I thought to myself.

He yanked his wallet out from his pocket and showed me a picture when he was indeed a monk with a shaved head, and deep orange robes adorning his much younger body.

"I grow hair after that. No cut ever."

"Can you fight?" That's something I always want to know.

"Ohhhh, yes," he said as if I asked a stupid question. "I fight good. I strong. Fight Muay Thai when young but stop cause feel bad for making people sleep. I no want to hurt people."

I couldn't contain myself and burst out laughing at his description of knocking someone out.

"What funny, silly girl?"

I tried to help him out with his slang reference: "I stopped fighting because I felt bad for knocking people out!"

"Yes, make them sleep."

I chuckled, gazing out of the tinted windows and thought once again, *You're definitely not in Kansas anymore, Dorthy...*

About ten minutes later we arrived to mobs of cars, motorbikes, and people coming and going from the wide-open, dark area that had been made into a parking lot. Thai Man let his window down, said a few things in Thai, handed a much smaller guy some money, and followed another man waving an orange flag to park. His stick-shift with all the fixings sounded like he was challenging someone to a race, no matter that we were only going five miles an hour. We parked and exited the car, walking towards the carnival. It became clear there were hordes of people, who were ALL Thai. We were making our way through a stuffy, tight crowd, so he got directly in front of me, wrapping my right hand around the back of his belt.

"Don't let go," he ordered.

I was considerably smaller than him, so people squeezing through and past us couldn't see me as they approached, but once they laid eyes on me, it was nothing but stares. Mouths dropped and folks stopped in their path or mid-sentence. Every ten seconds, he would ask, "You okay?" while grabbing back for my arm.

I was more than okay. I was completely at peace and happy for no reason at all, surrounded by staring people in a foreign land, all speaking a language that was as foreign as this man I was holding onto. But somehow the land and the man seemed like exactly where I was supposed to be, and strangely familiar.

When we finally made it through the crowd to an open area, he immediately grabbed my hand with so much intention. For the first time I was slightly self-conscious, because everyone was staring at us. I didn't know if it was because his hair was so long, or because I was an alien they had never seen before. As women passed by, they looked at him, then looked at me. I quickly learned that Thai women thought I was "sexy," which they equated with "beautiful." I will blame the English-speaking men who come and objectify Thai women for that mix-up. A few would say, "You berry sexyyy." The first couple times my eyes got big, and I laughed, because I didn't know how to respond. Thai Man loved all the attention coming my way. It was amusing watching him amused. He bought some tickets and pulled me to the Ferris wheel. I was excited to escape the piercing stares for the ten minutes we made the loop, but it was soon back to reality.

After riding a few more rides, we walked over to a concert, which was on the other side of the park. As we stood in the crowd, I was tickled pink because the Thai singer was doing his best Usher-inspired R&B

performance, and he was obviously a Thai star. Hearing the classic R&B runs, melody, and tones sung in Thai reminded me that black culture travels across the world in a way we don't even recognize. I guarantee seventy-five percent of these people had never, and I mean never, seen a black person up close and in person, yet here they were enjoying black culture. Thai Man started singing the song, in Thai, at the top of his lungs with his arms raised. "Is this real life?!" I blurted out loud. I thought I was a free spirit, but compared to him, I was Whitley Gilbert, who was an uppity character from a beloved show from my childhood, *A Different World*. He was like an intense breath of fresh air. It made me uncomfortable but in awe at the same time.

After about thirty minutes, he grabbed my hand, saying, "Time for eat." I told him all my food restrictions as he dragged me to the food section of the carnival. After going to a number of different vendors and collecting various things into a couple of bags, he grabbed my hand and said, "Pa!" We walked and walked until he found a grassy area where there weren't many people. He was pleased. Pulling out a majestic, beautiful piece of material he had just bought, he laid it out and told me to sit. The Whitley Gilbert in me pulled out some hand sanitizer, putting some in both our hands. Before I knew it, I was being fed an array of different things while his eyes were glued to mine, waiting for each reaction. I have an extremely expressive face, which thrilled him with all the different twists and turns of my lips, eyes, and nose as each piece of food invoked a different portrait.

If you had told me a year ago that I would be sitting in the grass in Thailand with a Thai man I'd met earlier that day while looking for fruit, and I would be eating Thai food after seeing a Thai Usher concert with him hours later, I would have laughed and looked at you like you were nuts. But my life had gotten stranger and stranger over the last couple of months... and I wasn't complaining one bit. I couldn't have made this up in my mind if I had wanted to, so I decided to live in the moment and pay attention to what the universe was saying to me. At that moment I was learning a lesson in being even more open than I'd thought I was, and free. Free to new experiences, free to whatever the universe sent my way, free to give up any notion of how things are *supposed to be.* Free to things being way better than I had imagined them. The art of just being. Taji was right—I was so stuck in the script I had created when it came to men. This was not part of that script.

***

I was minding my own business the next day when I got a voice message on WhatsApp: "I done working for now, I go back later. I come get you go to mountain for couple hours." Hiking, mountains, sunsets, trees, and nature are my sweet spot! You can't dangle that in my face and not get me excited.

When most people think of Thailand, they think of the picturesque islands and beaches in the south or the hustle and bustle of Bangkok. But much farther up north, tucked away in the mountains, you'll find Chiang Mai with sunsets that rival those anywhere on the planet. Temples and more temples are everywhere you look, with monks all around. It feels different. It has the perfect blend of city life while holding onto the authentic spirit and culture of the people of northern Thailand. If you drive out of the city into the little nooks and crannies, you are quickly taken back 100 years, where it is absolutely nothing like city life, and nobody speaks English. I was about to find out how much I loved the dichotomy.

An hour after that message, I was back in the fast-and-furious car, going for my first of many hikes in the mountains and jungles of Chiang Mai Province. This would become one of our *things,* once he realized how happy it made me. Going with Thai Man on these adventures was different than any hiking experience I'd had before; it was like going with Mowgli from *The Jungle Book* or Tarzan. Somehow he knew every spider, every plant and its healing property, every insect and fruit, and when it was going to rain. He could open a coconut with nothing but his hands and could make tightly coiled plants do magical things like spring open. Butterflies landed on this man's shoulder. It was like something out of a freaking Disney movie. He was in sync with nature in a way I'd never witnessed.

Our first hike was when I discovered a squat toilet for the first time. We had been hiking for a couple of hours, and I drank quite a bit of water along the way. I had to pee! Bad. Thank goodness this was an actual trail that had a toilet close to the exit. I approached the wooden box structure that was the restroom. When I opened the door, I found a primitive bathroom. To my surprise, this was unlike any toilet I'd ever used before; it was just a toilet-esque looking thing pretty much on the ground... no flush, just a big basin filled with water and a bucket next to it. *What in the…?*

I came out of the bathroom and said to him, "Umm, I have no clue how to use this bathroom."

He laughed and laughed and laughed, opening the door. Then he demonstrated as he lectured.

"You squat, and you pee goes down. Then you get water with bucket, pour it, and pee goes down drain."

After he went back out, I still just stood with a puzzled look for another three minutes, looking at the dirt floor. Being that I'm a former dancer and squat over every public toilet seat anyway, I thought, *I should be able to aim my pee so I don't make a mess.* But

I knew it was so low on the ground, anything could go wrong! What if my pee decided it wanted to zigzag and got on my clothes or something? *Should I just take my pants off to be sure?*

At this point I really had to go, so I went for it.

I pulled my pants way down while straddling the squat toilet, each leg on a different side. I set myself back in a squat position, used my hand to hold my pants forward, and went for it.

"Please, pee, just go straight down," I said as though it were a mantra.

Luckily, I didn't make a mess. It was a bring-your-own-toilet-paper situation, and I was extremely happy the Whitley Gilbert in me always carries wet wipes. I was slightly traumatized for the next minute, then laughed, imagining what my friends, mom, and sister would have to say about my first squat toilet experience. That was the first of many squat toilets I would come across, and now I knew what to do... somewhat.

When I got home, I took a shower and immediately went to sleep, wondering what would be next.

***

Thai massages had become a staple for me. They were the best massages in the world, and only $5 a piece, which meant I was getting one every other day at a minimum. One particular day, I was headed to get a massage with Thai Man at his favorite place. We got there, and he hugged an older woman while pointing to me. She smiled, calling me "sexy girl" while touching my face and handing me some clothes to change into. All the masseuses loved giving me massages. Thai massages stretch your entire body out. You will find the masseuse in between your legs with one of your legs up on her shoulder while she's pushing it back towards your head. Being a ballerina and dancer for twelve years until the age of twenty meant I was still quite flexible, plus I do yoga.

They loved pushing my body to the limit to see how far my legs, hips, arms, and back could be twisted and pulled. The old lady smiled in excitement letting out a "woah" as she pushed my leg until I was in a full split. I felt like I'd just had an amazing chiropractic visit when leaving; I was floating on cloud nine.

Outside were some food vendors in a small market. Thai Man eats grilled bug like snacks, and, somehow, I accepted the challenge of eating one. His favorite "bug lady" had some freshly cooked bugs waiting for him. He purchased ten, excited for me to try one, sure I would love them as much as he did.

We sat on the steps as he pulled the insect out of the plastic bag… it was huge! Not believing I had agreed to do this, I grimaced, trying to figure out what the heck it even was. I figured out it was a cricket. A big, seasoned, grilled cricket!

"Eat all!" he instructed as he lunged the cricket towards my mouth.

I took a healthy bite and started chewing. *It's not half bad,* I was thinking when he proceeded to tell me, "Chew all, because it have egg in here…"

What did he mean there were eggs in it?! Oh hell to the no.

I began to spit out the cricket as he screamed, "No no no no!"

I couldn't believe I was eating a bug!

"It's good, no?" he said hopefully.

I didn't reply.

"Babe, it's good?" he questioned.

"No! It's a bug!" was all I could muster, still not believing I had just eaten a poor little cricket. I chugged down a bottle of water and went to get some sweet corn from one of the stands to erase my experience and remind me of home. He finished the rest of the crickets himself.

When he dropped me back off at home, he told me he had a surprise for me that weekend. I couldn't wait to see what it could be...

10

MAKE IT STOP!

Sweetest thing I've ever known.
Was like the kiss on the collarbone."

~Lauryn Hill

We were going on a new adventure every day it seemed. Next up was his surprise — camping in the mountains. He had the bright idea that we should drive an hour plus outside the city to a camp site that had a decent number of other campers, so that's where we were headed. I laughed at everything he wanted to listen to during the drive. He didn't have a clue who Jay-Z, Jay Electronica, Erykah Badu, or Nina Simone were, so thank God we finally had a musical breakthrough discovering that we both loved Michael Jackson. I am a Michael fanatic, so singing all the songs at the top of my lungs while taking in my surroundings was not a problem. He would sing certain parts, but mostly he let me entertain him by being my crazy self, doing a full-out concert, including front-seat dancing for every single song. He laughed and laughed. At one point, he pulled over to get something to drink from a small store. When I saw him coming back, I hopped out of the car and turned the music up. I did the moonwalk into my MJ spin, something I've been doing since I was five years old, and maaaan, was I *on* that particular day. He started screaming, "Oh! Oh! Oh! You moonwalk! You look like Michael Jackson! How you make you feet do that?!" He began trying to imitate me. He looked completely ridiculous, and I laughed until I was bent over and my stomach was hurting. I stumbled back into the car, still laughing uncontrollably, and we continued our journey to the camp site.

We finally arrived, and of course I was the only non-Thai person within miles. I couldn't believe my first time sleeping in a real, old-school style tent was going to be in Thailand. My dad bought me an army green tent when I was about seven or eight, but I chickened out every time we were going to actually use it. I did learn how to set it up in my grandmother's backyard, though. We set up shop quickly, and I was eager to walk around before it was too dark. We took a long walk as I oooohhed and awwwwed at the sky, which looked completely different as the backdrop to this other world I had just entered. He told me he'd protect me from tigers if they came out, and I laughed, thinking he was joking—but I still don't quite know if he was. The mountains were majestic, and the sunset was like something out of a dream you'd want to remember for eternity. It was finally dark, and there was no turning back now. I was officially camping... in Thailand!

We sat outside the tent looking at the stars and talking for hours. It was amazing how comfortable I felt with someone I technically had so little in common with. We all have special superpowers, and one of mine is that I can connect easily, deeply, and quickly with all types of people. But this was different. We naturally just got one another, so hanging out for extended periods of time was pure chilled fun. It was chilly once the sun went down, and I was extremely relieved he'd told me to pack warm clothing, plus he brought me extra things to stay warm. He saw some other campers a ways down who had a fire going and a guitar. "Pa," he said, jumping up.

I was perfectly content in the little world we had created and didn't really want to go and sit with random strangers who most likely wouldn't understand a word I was saying. Then I thought, *When is the next time this will happen?* Up we went to make our way to their camp, where they had food, a fire, and drinks. Thai Man can make friends with anyone, and I mean anyone, in under ten seconds. The campers were laughing and telling us to have a seat immediately, offering us a million things, in Thai of course, after he said a couple of things to them. They tried their best not to stare at me. The guitar player, who actually spoke decent English, asked me to sing. I told him I didn't know anything he was playing, and he let me know he loved American music by going through song after song until surprisingly, he started playing something I actually loved—Lauryn Hill's (originally Roberta Flack's) "Killing Me Softly." He sang along while he was playing and sounded pretty dope.

The one thing I can do pretty well is harmonize, so I immediately started singing with him to everyone's amazement, which doubled when I harmonized the notes at the perfect time. Chillll. You would've thought I was Erykah Badu up in that joint, the way they all looked enchanted. Next, he started playing Lorde's "Royal." I couldn't believe it and had an out-of-body experience.

I chuckled, thinking the only reason I knew that song was because of my time in Hawaii. After my solo time on the island, my best friend Regina came with some family and friends and had a beautiful wedding. That was the entire reason I had gone alone to Hawaii the week before her wedding. She, her husband, his best man, and I got into the car to go hiking and whatever else, and without fail, every single time, that song came on the radio. It happened so much we started calling it our Hawaii soundtrack and theme song, singing along like we were in a video—well, Regina and I did, because she's just as

149

dramatic as I am. Of course we'd met in our performing arts middle school.

It was a full-circle cipher moment. I was way up in the mountains of Thailand, camping in a tent for the first time in my life, with a bunch of Thai people, singing the song that was the soundtrack of one of the defining times of my life that had actually led to this moment. That feeling of énouement crept in, and I wished I could tell my former self this story.

Thai Man and I finally made our way back to our camp after I gave him a look. Funny how he knew from a simple glance I was ready to go. I felt like I was living in three of my favorite books all at once in real life. *The Alchemist*, *Eat Pray Love*, and the *Midnight* series by Sister Souljah. Those were books I'd read a million times, and somehow I had manifested a gumbo of them into a real-life experience.

We were now comfortably back to our tent, and I was in a state of overwhelming appreciation. After staring me in the eyes for a few seconds, I was caught totally off guard when he kissed me for the first time. I immediately started crying! What a first kiss, huh? I am not a crier, yet I was weeping like a baby. Not knowing why I was crying made it worse; I was thoroughly confused. He didn't say anything at all, putting me in his lap, rocking and holding me like a baby. As my face was smashed into his chest, I could smell his oil and skin through his t-shirt, which was now soaked wet from my ongoing stream of tears. I kept thinking to myself, *What the heck is going on?! Stop it. Make it stop! Somebody make me stop crying.* But I couldn't, no matter how much I tried. It was as if everything ever hidden beneath the layers of defenses, numbness, and veneers was being released. And for some reason he didn't question it, wasn't afraid of it, and embraced it. He embraced me. He didn't try to make it better, he let me *just be.*

During those three minutes, I think I experienced every human emotion, and it was intense. Finally, I surrendered and allowed the pain that had been suppressed—every insecurity, every fear, every rejection, every hidden part that wanted to be acknowledged—spill over and find their way out. His drenched shirt, his healing hands, empathetic spirit, and protective energy absorbed it all.

Cleanse.

Release.

Let go.

A well-needed piece of freedom was on the other side. I slept better than I had in years.

11

RUN FOR THE BORDER!

But today I got my thoroughest girl with me.
I'm mashin' the gas, she grabbin' the wheel,
it's trippy, how hard she rides with me...

~Jay Z

Sooner than later, my one-month visa was up, and I had to make a decision. Was I going to stay longer? My original plan was to spend a month in Thailand, then a month in Bali, but I wasn't quite done with Thailand yet for a number of reasons. I decided I was going to make a border run to the neighboring country, Myanmar, previously known as Burma, which travelers wanting to extend their stay in Thailand often did. It came up on me so quickly, and it seemed pretty straightforward. Thai Man wanted to take a trip to the neighboring country of Laos, where I could apply for a three-month visa at the Thai embassy, but I had it in my mind I was not going to need three more months in Thailand. I did some quick internet research and booked a VIP bus to Myanmar, leaving the next morning. It was supposed to be simple—I would cross the border, spend some time in Myanmar, then when I was ready to come back, I'd enter Thailand again on a new one-month visa. I'd get back on the VIP bus and come back to Chiang Mai. Nice. Simple. Easy.

Thai Man took me to the bus station, pleading with me that he should come. "The bus can be bbbbery dangerous. They drive crazy up in mountains!"

"No. I'm a big girl. I'll be fine. Trust me," I kept responding.

"Bus can be dangerous! Sometimes bus drives fast up in mountains and crash." He warned me with all the concern in the world as his eyes got big.

I had it in my mind I was going alone; I was due for a solo adventure. The way this VIP bus worked, you booked your ticket and a specific seat in advance on a website, like an airplane. I had picked a window seat that was in an empty row at the time of my purchase. I had no clue if someone had booked the seat next to me since then.

We arrived at the bus station and located my bus. He said a couple things to the bus attendant, the equivalent of a flight attendant, and proceeded to get onto the bus with me, walking me to my seat. There were only Thai people staring at me and a couple of monks sitting in the front. We got to my seat, and I felt like a child whose father was dropping her off for her first day of school. He made sure I was buckled in and my bags were secure.

"Be careful, okay?" he said sternly but with concern.

"I will. Don't worry. I'll be fine!" I tried to soothe him. I could tell it didn't work.

He got off the bus and stood outside my window like a parent at a bus stop. As I was looking at him through the window, admiring his concern and rolling my eyes at the same time, a young, racially ambiguous woman sat next to me. We smiled at one another, both noticing we were the only non-Thai people on the entire bus other than an Italian family that was now in the front with a Thai woman. The attendant said some things in Thai, and the bus pulled off. Thai Man stood outside, mouthing "Be careful" as I made my way on a new solo adventure.

The bus zipped through the mountains at a speed I can guarantee was not for the faint of heart, and a couple times I indeed thought I might die. We came to a random stop, and some official-looking uniformed men got on the bus. Everyone started removing their passports or paperwork from their pockets and purses and opening their bags to be searched. The girl sitting next to me looked at me; we had the same "Are we about to get arrested?" face. It was at that moment we noticed we both had American passports and said "same same" in unison.

"Same same" is a casual expression used in Thailand that means exactly what it says, same same. The official-looking men saw that we both had American passports and didn't look too hard at our things or paperwork like they did everyone else on the bus. It was like something in a movie. To our surprise, this kind of stop happened randomly three more times.

"I had no clue where you were from!" I said to my new American friend.

"I know, I was waiting for you to say something, because I didn't know if you spoke English either," she confessed. "I was born in Iran but moved to the States when I was two. I live in Atlanta."

"What are the chances we randomly chose seats next to each other? That's crazy," I said, knowing this was another synchronistic moment I couldn't have planned.

"That is soooooo bizarre!" she agreed.

We both felt better knowing we at least had each other when it was time to cross the land border — that is, if we got through the bus ride alive. During the one rest stop, the squat toilets were so archaic that we waited for one another outside the bathroom. This way we could hold each other's belonging and not have to bring them inside the less than desirable bathroom and set them down on anything. I always carry tons of Clorox wipes, baby wipes, and toilet paper—I grabbed them out of my backpack, and we used the Clorox wipes to wipe the bottoms of our shoes before getting back on the bus.

A few hours later we arrived at our final stop in the Thai-Myanmar border town on the Thai side, and we exited the bus with our belongings. It was hot and humid. We needed to find a tuk-tuk, a motorized rickshaw, to get us to the border, so off we went to hail one. The tuk-tuk we finally got onto was packed. We kept giggling and looking at each other as more and more people got on. Eventually one man was even hanging on the back. It was an interesting ride, but we arrived. We figured out where to go and approached the guarded booth at the crossing. I handed the border patrol man my passport and was surprised when he handed it back, saying sternly and slowly, "No leave."

My eyes got big as I said, "Why no leave?"

"Ahhhhh, no, ahhh time. Come back. You stay Myanmar." It took him two minutes to get that much out, as his English was minimal.

He pointed to a sign; we deciphered that they had just changed the rules two days before. They were no longer allowing border runs at this crossing for the time being. My visa was expiring the next day, and the kind patrol officer knew they wouldn't let me back into Thailand on a new visa if I crossed into Myanmar; he didn't want me to get stuck there. I began having a mini heart attack. My new friend handed him her passport and asked, "Same same?" She had a multiple-entry work visa because she was teaching English under a program, so she was good to go. He stamped her passport and told her it was okay. She looked like she wanted to cry, "I don't want to leave you and don't want to go by myself either!"

It's funny in these situations how quickly you get attached to people who were complete strangers only hours before. Time is irrelevant, and it's like you're in a movie with extremely quick character and relationship development. I was still in slight shock, realizing that as of the next day I would be in Thailand illegally. I was having an out-of-body experience with the humid heat beating down my back, and I needed food. I wasn't thinking straight and bugging out in my mind.

"I'm stuck in Burma, what am I going to do?!" I said to my new friend in a panic.

She laughed and reminded me, "You're still in Thailand!"

We both began laughing hysterically, breaking the heaviness of the moment as I said, "Oh yeah. Duuuhhh."

We gave each other hugs, and off she went.

From the Italian man who had been on the VIP bus, I found out there was a Thai embassy a couple of miles away. I decided to try my luck and see if I could renew my visa there before heading back to the bus station and trying to catch a bus back to Chiang Mai. I didn't want to catch the bus the next day with an expired visa, risking discovery by the scary officers getting on and inspecting passports. It meant I had to make sure I got on a bus that evening if I didn't have a new visa.

I arrived at the embassy after catching a motorcycle taxi, which was weird. Riding on the back of a motorcycle with a person I didn't know was not my ideal situation, but desperate times called for desperate measures. I arrived at the embassy only to find out the only place I could extend my visa for a month was at the local consulate—guess where? Chiang Mai! I thought to myself, *You said you were due an adventure; you should be careful what you wish for.* Making my way back to the bus station, I was hot, sweaty from running around, and not looking forward to the bus ride back to Chiang Mai, where I had just come from. At that moment I wished I'd actually hung out with some Americans, who might have known this information about the changing rules or local consulate. I could have saved myself a trip.

I sent Thai Man a voice note, and he sent one back saying, "It be okay. I take you to consulate first thing morning. No problem. I know someone there." Waiting at the bus station after buying some local street food, I sat and thought to myself that even in the midst of a wasted trip, it was freaking cool. I mean, I was here alone at the border of Thailand and the former Burma, getting turned away at a border crossing.

A couple hours later, it was finally time to go. I was excited to get on the air-conditioned bus after the day I'd had. I slept most of the bus ride, and after hours and hours weaving through the mountains once again, the bus finally pulled up to the bus station in Chiang Mai. It was the dead of the night, but right where he'd left me at the crack of dawn that morning, there was Thai Man with a grin, excitedly awaiting my arrival. I couldn't help but laugh as I was getting off; you would have thought he hadn't seen me in a week.

He hugged me and asked, "You okay? You okay?"

As soon as I said yes, he said, "We go eat, you need eat."

The next day we made a trip to the consulate. After four hours of paperwork and waiting, my stay was extended another month, which meant I was not in Thailand illegally.

12

ENOUGH

Everything I'm not, made me everything

I am!

~Kanye West

I spent some daylight hours each day exploring the numerous peaceful, beautiful, majestic temples all over Chiang Mai. What a sight to see. The various colors painted throughout each unique structure always had gold weaving through them, and they brought a certain calm to my spirit. I found one in particular that made me just feel good every time I entered. I would spend thirty minutes to an hour daily in contemplation and meditation there. Sometimes the monks were around with their quiet presence, or stragglers would come in and out. But mostly, I was alone.

My mind would race for a few minutes, sometimes many minutes, going over anything and everything you can imagine, on autopilot. Instead of making the mistake of forcing myself to "always think positive," I decided not to compete with myself, my thoughts, or my feelings and let them naturally flow through me, actively witnessing them. No judgement. I took mental notes of different triggers, and they became the things for me to journal about and explore.

In the temples, I always eventually found my breath and my mind chatter would start to slow down. I had never in my life taken the time to just be.

It dawned on me that we are born with a perfect, blank canvas. We are all born connected directly to God, untainted; we trust naturally. Why wouldn't we? As we go through life, we are programmed by everything around us, and we *forget*.

I had forgotten.

So much of my self-worth was caught up in doing, striving, having, comparing, achieving, giving, giving, giving — I had *forgotten* the beautiful art of simply being. I had *forgotten* how to receive. I had *forgotten* that perfection is not the answer, and my need for perfection was rooted in the fear of not being good enough. The fear of not being good enough led me to massive miscalculations concerning my self-worth that I had measured myself against.

I had a deep-seated need to prove my worth and earn my value. The light within hit me, so "I am enough" was the mantra I naturally locked in on as I breathed in, breathing out everything in my cells telling me differently. In this Buddhist temple, I began to believe it.

I apologized to myself, then offered her forgiveness.

***

A few weeks later Thai Man looked at me and smiled. "I love you. Easy to love you. Easy to be around. You no bark at me. I comfortable around you. I say anything what I think, and you no judge me. You energy calm me. You make me feel. You small girl but power like tiger. You no talk much, but everything you say important. You best girl in world!"

I blushed with a smile from ear to ear at his endearing proclamation and assessment. I didn't need a savior. I also didn't need someone to tell me how pretty I was, how talented, or how smart. All those things were lovely to hear, and he couldn't get enough of telling me every chance he got, but I didn't need it. I needed someone who, being in my presence, felt and recognized the otherness that even I couldn't describe. I needed someone who could sense the chaos going on inside my head, look up from his book, place his hand on my head, and simply say "Calm down, small girl, calm down," then go right back to reading without questioning me. It was eerie the way he sensed me.

He didn't like me because of the hundreds of things we had in common, because technically we only had a few. I believe I could have shown him the worst version of myself 24/7, and somehow he would have still seen something beautiful. He was interested and in awe of *me*. The me who was there, no matter how triggered I was or how silent I became.

He craved my essence and wanted my soul next to his. It's easy for me to hide the deeper parts of who I am, but for some reason, I couldn't hide from him and didn't want to. I was exposed... but safe. I was Noni and he was Shabazz from *Beyond the Lights*, and I felt seen. It's funny how the simple act of being seen allowed me to just *be* even more.

He wasn't afraid of how he felt about me, even if he saw the fire in my eyes. It was a blaze he was willing to walk through with no hesitation or second thoughts. He made me fall in love with myself more and more by allowing me to see myself through his untainted, unobstructed view. I was awakened simply by the way he looked at me. I understood on a deeper level that I am enough.

He graduated from Thai Man to Thai Bae.

***

Thai Bae was a hustler; he loved to work and work and work some more. He was a true entrepreneur who lived and breathed working. He had a side business that started taking up a ton of his time—buying and selling farms up in the mountains,

167

as well as shipping and selling fruit from some of these farms in bulk. I didn't mind him working all the time, because I actually needed the space and solitude. Just about every free second he had he devoted to me, which wasn't much but just enough. He would work, work, work and somehow just know I hadn't eaten. I always ate a large lunch, then I would get so caught up in working, reading, staring at the sky, and other things, that I'd forget to eat dinner.

At 9:00 or 10:00 p.m., there would be a knock on the door. He would enter with a huge smile and FOOD. In Thailand when you get food to go, it's called "take away." No matter if it's soup, rice, or something with gravy, you get it in a clear plastic bag like a ziplock but thicker, and the top is wrapped with a rubber band to ensure it doesn't spill out.

I would tell him I wasn't hungry, sometimes half sleep, but he would still prepare the food in a bowl and feed me until I ate. No matter how many hours he worked, he would immediately make me Thai tea. I can assure you, he made the best Thai tea in all of Thailand, perfecting it to my liking after finding out the old woman in the alley made it better than him.

Little things like that made me appreciate him and melt in his presence. I would tell him not to make me any tea because he needed to rest, and he would repeat every time, "You clean my house me no ask, you get my clothes clean, you go to post office for me and send packages, plus you make me happy. I can make you Thai tea every day, no problem."

He was bold, sometimes brash, and he said whatever came to his mind, but he was thoughtful. A lot of people mistake politeness for thoughtfulness, but they are two totally different things. He was exactly who he appeared to be, which is something I always appreciate in a person. He paid attention and then instinctively thought of ways to make me smile.

Most nights we would visit some Thai restaurant that I would never have visited if not for him. Small places tucked away in Thai neighborhoods with nothing but Thai being spoken. I rarely ordered my own food when he was around, which was okay, because he knew what I liked. He would place an order, then a ton of food would appear. He'd finish off his own food and then finish off whatever his best friend, Dave, who often came with us, and I didn't eat. Dave (his nickname) spoke almost no English. Thai Bae would force us to eat until we literally couldn't eat anymore. We'd just look at each other and give a non-verbal "here we go" look. If you were around him, you would be well-nourished, that's for sure.

One of the first things Dave said to me when we met was, "You hair big like lion!"

I laughed and laughed as he smiled, happy with what he deemed a compliment.

Thai Bae immediately hit back, "Dave you mouth like a dog!"

Dave's face twisted as Thai Bae immediately laughed, "Same same as her hair, like lion, no?"

Dave smacked himself in the head, getting that he hadn't given me a compliment, although I thought the comparison was hilarious and accurate.

Every day Thai Bae and I became closer and closer. We created our own little universe in this foreign land that was becoming more and more familiar by the moment. I'd often wake up in the death grip of his big biceps across my torso holding me so close that our breath had no choice but to sync.

I'd lie there and wonder if I spoke fluent Thai in his dreams. The sound of what seemed like a million variations of birds singing and greeting me reminded me every morning to trust the universal thread and soul of life. Before the sun had actually risen, the birds and roosters were excited to start their day at the crack of dawn, trusting the sun was on its way. I would look over, and how long he had been in the sun determined how deep his gorgeous skin was glowing. Thai people are melanated, although most advertisements show them having very fair skin. Especially up north in the mountains, their skin can have deep, dark, rich tones with red undertones. Absolutely gorgeous. I can still remember the first time he took his shirt off in front of me. We were hiking, and he found a body of water, at which point he literally stripped down to his underwear. It revealed two things, the tattoo that covered his entire back and that his nipples were a deep dark brown.

I was living in Thailand, falling in love with a Thai Man. I had to pinch myself all the time to make sure I was not dreaming. My reality had become so beautiful but far from what I had expected… the one thing it was, was soulful.

13

ROAD TRIPPING

Somebody told me that this planet was small...

~Black Thought

Two months had passed, and it was time for me to either leave Thailand or go to a neighboring country, Laos, where I could apply for a three-month visa at the Thai embassy. My anxiety was building up because the entire process sounded exhausting. Going to an embassy sounded so formal, and I couldn't wait until it was over. What if I couldn't get a visa? Would they let me back into Thailand?

Thai Bae was excited to go on a road trip and insisted we drive. By driving, we could explore Laos, and he could show me around. He decided we should take Chinese Bruce, a tall, handsome Chinese guy we had met a couple weeks before. He was now Thai Bae's adopted brother. Bruce had been living in Thailand the past year, and Thai Bae met him when he decided to sell one of his cars and Bruce bought it. They were inseparable after that.

The first time Bruce and I met, I could tell he was shocked that Thai Bae's girlfriend was a black American girl—his face gave it away. He was shy and blushing at everything I said, but it wasn't long before he got really comfortable with me. Despite his limited English, we just vibed. We vibed so much that when his younger eighteen-year-old sister was in town and he needed to leave on a business trip to southern Thailand, he asked me to hang out with her, really to babysit her for the day. That's a later story. Language, culture, and ethnicity can never replace energy. Energy speaks in ways words cannot because people can feel each other without any words being spoken.

My eight years working as a college counselor had allowed me to deal closely and intimately with people from every kind of background. I learned that energy trumps everything because "people will always remember how you made them feel," as the great Maya Angelou put it. When a person has restrictive energy, it's much harder to connect with them beyond differences. But when someone's energy is open and curious, it can penetrate, allowing a certain level of comfort to be established rather quickly with no rhyme or reason.

We were all gearing up to leave in the infamous sports car. I was somewhat dreading the twelve-hour drive to Laos, but I'd get to see more of Thailand on the way, which was always a good thing. My body was draping the back seat; I was elated that Bruce was there to keep Thai Bae company so I could sleep when I wanted, listen to podcasts, and daze off into daydreams as I often do. Once we were hours out of the city, there was nothing but old-school squat toilets when we stopped.

At one point, Thai Bae was on the phone talking to someone in Thai while Bruce was on the phone talking to someone in Chinese. I couldn't help but let out a laugh. My life was getting more and more bizarre by the minute. I mean... Here I was driving to Laos in the fast-and-furious car with a Thai man who had just met a Chinese man a few weeks before, and

I knew neither of them two months ago. Somehow it all seemed perfectly normal at that point. That feeling of énouement crept in again: the bitter-sweetness of arriving in the future, but not being able to go back and tell your past self how it ends up. I wanted so badly to go back to the former version of me who was reading the email that shattered her world and to let her know she hadn't even begun to know the magic to come.

Id say:

"Feel it all, don't resist it. Swim into the darkness below the shallow water of your consciousness, dive deep. Find the bottom of the ocean; there are some weeds there. Dig through the sand and pull up the root of those weeds, my dear. Breathe, you have an oxygen mask on... breathe some more. Bless the weeds and tell them you see them. You've felt them begging to be uprooted but ignored them because you thought you'd drown if you followed the path of darkness to get to them. Breathe some more to remind yourself you have an oxygen mask on. Swim back towards the sunlight. There's so much more awaiting you above water; you can come up for fresh air now."

The weeds represented the fear of abandonment, rejection, and a false sense of security; all hiding behind my ego that put on a song and dance in many different ways. My attachment to that song and dance which kept me safe, wouldn't allow me to see how I was holding myself back from the magic that awaited. By not addressing my subconscious beliefs and pain, I wasn't able to fully embody who I really am. I could clearly see that now that I was on the other side.

Thai Bae peeked at me through the rear-view mirror, obviously entangled in my energy. Our eyes met as he squinted and said, "Small girl, energy powerful like a tiger." I smiled then immediately looked away, knowing the longer we locked eyes, the more he'd know my thoughts. He stretched his arm back and rubbed my leg. I drifted back to sleep.

Twelve exhausting hours later, we finally made it to the border. Now we had to get visas to enter the country, as well as some extra paperwork and fees to get the car through. We paid a man to handle all the paperwork for us, and while he was working everything out, we found a restaurant a couple doors down. With his good looks and likable personality, Thai Bae immediately charmed the waitress. I just laughed at how Thai women, and women in general would blush at him. I couldn't understand a word they were saying, but I always knew he was telling them I was his girlfriend because they'd end up saying, "Ohhhhhhhhhh!" looking at me with big eyes. If they knew some English, they'd say, "So pretty so pretty!" or "Sexy girl sexy girl wow! You lucky boy!"

Bruce and I sat on stand-by, anticipating what he ordered, knowing whatever would be presented to us would be full of flavor. We were correct! We dug in, and as we were finishing our meal, the visa man interrupted us to let us know we were ready to cross the border. We gathered our things, collected the paperwork from him, and proceeded to the border control booth. Thirty-five minutes later, we were through my first successful land border crossing in a car, and we were driving towards Vientiane, Laos.

Lao and Thai are two different but similar languages. Thai Bae could speak and understand it minimally but more than enough to communicate and get directions. It was like an English-speaker going to Jamaica and communicating with someone in Patois—you can figure it out; it may just take you a while.

We stopped by the Thai embassy, thinking we could get my paperwork in to be processed, but we found out they only accepted applications in the morning. It was Friday, and Monday was a Thai holiday, so we'd have to wait until Tuesday to submit the application. While at the embassy, we met a French man who was having a hard time communicating with the officials. The Thai women and men working at the embassy spoke Thai and a little English, neither of which this French man spoke or understood. Luckily for him, Thai Bae could translate French to Thai for them. Whenever he spoke French, Spanish, or Portuguese I was immediately hypnotized. Had he known the languages before his twenties, it would have been impressive in itself, but the fact he taught himself those and English on his own later in life and could speak all fluently absolutely blew my mind. *I've got to stop being a stuck-up English speaker and learn some more languages, man,* I always thought to myself. The French man was thankful and gave Thai Bae the biggest hug and handshake as a token of his appreciation.

Bruce and I were beyond tired, but Thai Bae insisted we take a two-to-three-hour drive up to Vang Vieng, which he deemed the most beautiful place. He was certain we could find a guesthouse when we got there, so reluctantly, we hopped back in the fast-and-furious car. I've learned to pick my battles with Alpha men carefully so that when I do have an issue or request, no matter how small it seems, I can expect it to be given the utmost respect and consideration. For this reason, I choose what I challenge and complain about... and this didn't seem worth it. He was excited, so I went along with his plan.

Once we got out of the city and started making our way up to Vang Vieng, way, way, up in the mountains, the roads were less than desirable. The bumps and holes were exponentially exaggerated in a low-riding, stick-shift sports car. The sun was beginning to set, and my head was beginning to hurt after the twelve-hour drive from Thailand, the couple of hours to get through the border, getting to the embassy, and now bump bump bump bump every other second. My irritation was beginning to set in on top of my anxiety of just wanting a new visa. Three hours had passed, and we were now winding and swerving in the dark on some of the steepest and craziest mountains I had ever driven through. The roads were getting worse and worse, so we had to drive at a pace close to crawling.

There were several times I was sure we were going to die or drive off the cliff—some of the long stretches of road had absolutely no light, plus there were no other cars. These were the kind of inclines and winding roads that should have the signs posted on roller coasters, warning you not to proceed if you take heart medication. Five hours into the ride, we still weren't there; I had a full-blown migraine, was hungry, and just wanted a dark room with a bed to go to sleep. We finally drove through a village, and I spoke up immediately, "Let's see if we can find a guesthouse nearby. I'm over this drive and I'm starving!"

Bruce immediately chimed in behind me, "Yes! Good! Good!"

Thai Bae tried to bully us, letting us know we were probably extremely close, but I can't be bullied, especially when I've already compromised. I needed food and sleep immediately. He pulled over and got out of the car to ask a Lao woman who was standing outside how close we were to Vang Vieng and where the closest guest house was. Bruce and I calculated while he was gone that what should have been a three-hour drive had already been five-plus, so even if he came back and said thirty minutes, that could mean ninety, and we were not with it! Luckily, when he got back in the car, he informed us there was a four-room guest house in this village just up the road, and the lady was calling the owner to let her know we were on our way. So that was the new plan.

Ten minutes later, we arrived at an adorable guesthouse that looked like four miniature row houses but were just simple connected rooms. We paid the lady in kip, the Lao currency, and went into the room. I had been holding my pee for the preceding two hours, so I ran into the bathroom and couldn't believe it was a squat toilet! I laughed because it was a nice squat toilet in a nicely tiled bathroom. It hit me: I was in some small village in Laos, and I definitely hadn't planned this. My head was on Level Explode at this point, so I finished, quickly showered, and changed my clothes.

We decided to walk through the village and find something to eat. Darkness filled the streets, but the main road on which we had driven to the guest house had some stores that looked like they might be open. In this village the structures were like going back 200-300 years in time or like something you'd see on TV in a third-world country documentary. I was walking far in front of the two men on this dark road; I had a slight attitude from being exhausted.

Thai Bae screamed out, "Slow down, small girl! It dark, I cannot see if something come out up there. We not home in Thailand."

Those words penetrated as I replayed them in my mind. *Woah! Did he just refer to my home as Thailand?* I didn't know how I felt about that in that moment; it just hit me like a ton of bricks. It was a surreal moment... I was walking down a dark street in a village in Laos, and my home was just referred to as Thailand. My mood immediately shifted, and I took in the moment. I wondered how many foreigners had walked down this exact road. I was guessing not many at all, being we were far off the tourist path. I looked up at the sky and realized I was seeing the moon literally halfway across the world in a spot I'd most likely never be again. I slowed down and let them catch up to me.

Thai Bae grabbed my neck and whispered in my ear, "I'm sorry, aye," kissing me on my forehead.

I let my irritation go at that moment and smiled.

About a block up the road, a car was approaching with bright lights. Bruce and Thai Bae simultaneously spotted a kitten in the middle of the street. Thai Bae darted into the street, grabbing the kitten, then running to the side of the road before the car hit them both. The little kitten was extremely weak, frail, and shaking as we huddled around the cute little baby. Bruce stripped off his tank top that was underneath his shirt to wrap around our new partner, now carrying her in his arms. We continued walking until we were in an area with storefronts and houses. We saw what looked like a place that served food, so Thai Bae ran inside to see if they were open. It was a mom-and-pop setup with some tables and mismatched plastic chairs spread out in the front of what we would consider a corner store at home. The young lady working there was extremely beautiful.

I couldn't help but say out loud, "Wow, you're gorgeous!"

She blushed as Thai Bae translated. She wanted to know what I was, as if I could possibly be an alien.

"She say she never see a person that look like you before," he said, laughing.

I was used to being stared at in Thailand by now, so it was like second nature, yet the stares in Laos were noticeably more intense. The people tended to be in pure shock, especially in the rural areas. Being in one of the few communist countries left in the world and a small village, the likelihood she had seen a black person before was slim, and her face expressed that. She kept pointing at my eyes, wanting to touch my hair, looking at me like I was a rare specimen.

This was a village that lived off the river, which meant we were eating fish. We had no other choice; it was the only thing on the menu. I had stopped eating pork and most red meat when I was thirteen and wasn't vegan yet, so fish sounded perfect to me. Little did I know I was about to be served the best fried fish my mouth had ever tasted. I guess when you eat fish every day, you learn how to cook it to perfection, and perfection was what these folks served. My grandmother on my mother's side is a fried fish expert with her deep southern roots. I grew up on Virginia spots seasoned well enough for any king. The fish I was served was seasoned well enough for a god!

By the time she put the fish and an array of sauces to complement it on the table, the entire family had come out to watch the night's entertainment...

which was ME! There were now sixteen eyes on me, watching my every move like I was the latest blockbuster film. The older lady at the table, whom I'm assuming was her grandmother, literally didn't take her eyes off of me once. Her mouth just hung like a swing on a swing-set, and her eyes stayed fixed on me with a hint of curiosity. If I smiled, they got excited; when I start singing and playing around with Bruce, they started clapping, and when I stood up to get a napkin they gasped, "Ahhhhh." I was completely embarrassed, but the fish was so good they could stare all they wanted, and I'd keep tearing it up. They were half as fascinated with Bruce, who is a handsome Chinese man with distinctly Chinese — not Thai or Lao — features. Bruce flashed his gorgeous smile, then kept his head down, eating, while focused on the new friend he had now claimed as his kitten. The kitten's name was now Sawadee, a take on the Thai greeting.

The waitress had grown quite fond of Thai Bae. I laughed. I didn't blame her; he is gorgeous and charming with a smile that lights up a room. The one thing I knew for certain is that he knew and valued what we had and wasn't the type of man to jeopardize that under any circumstance. He knew that I just rolled my eyes and laughed at the attention he got. He always wondered why I never called him or texted him a million times, didn't ask where he was, and didn't mind him going out with his friends alone when I didn't want to go.

"You never bark at me!" he always said.

I knew he didn't have the ability to lie or keep the truth from me. In fact, he told the truth to an extent that was annoying. "I don't like that lipstick!" "You're going to leave me for bwack guy with big bwack dick!" Anytime he'd fart, he'd tell me before he did it—he literally said whatever came to his mind. He said he was only that free with me because I never judged him and made him feel comfortable, but I can't imagine him saying anything but exactly what he was thinking, no matter who it was. He was usually a good sport when men stared at me. He would actually say, "She beautiful, right?" when people would gawk at me for extended periods of time, which made me uncomfortable. Half the time I didn't notice anyone staring. But he had a possessive side that I did not like, and he could be extremely insecure. It came out when he started randomly telling people we were getting married soon and would be having a baby after that. At first it was funny when I thought he was joking, but then I realized he was dead ass serious. It wasn't funny anymore.

We finished our food and picked up water and things for the cat to eat from the attached "store" and went on our way. Everyone in the family smiled and clapped as I waved and thanked them for their hospitality. I couldn't wait to get to sleep.

Unfortunately, the next morning, my head was still killing me. Since Vang Vieng is so high up in the mountains, the temperature drops when the sun is not out, and it becomes cool. I just wanted to stay under the covers in the dark.

"What you want to eat? You need eat," Thai Bae rolled over and said.

"We can just go back to that place we ate yesterday, if that's okay with you," I responded.

While I showered in the bathroom with the squat toilet, he went to check on Bruce and the new feline addition to the crew, Sawadee. By the time he returned, I had all of our things neatly packed and ready to go. We returned to the small restaurant, and guess what was on the menu again for breakfast? Fried fish. My taste buds started watering as I anticipated that seasoning that tasted like someone's auntie from New Orleans had been in the kitchen. The local village children were up and out and beautiful as can be. Two little boys in particular stood and looked at us with curiosity. We bought a bunch of candy, passing it out to them and their friends, which made their day.

That was just like Thai Bae... everywhere we went, he was feeding stray dogs, giving people money, or passing out candy. I remembered one day back in Thailand, we went to a local coffee village with a young French couple we had just met. He was so excited at the chance to speak French for the day, plus he wanted to show them the real Chiang Mai and Thailand. When we got to the coffee village, he bought enough candy from the local corner store for every kid to have a few pieces. There were at least thirty kids lining the dirt road, excited by the candy and foreign faces coming through.

This village we were currently in, in Laos was a place the people seemed content, smiling, and strikingly beautiful. Lao women are extremely easy on the eyes, with naturally full, gorgeous lips, broad noses, and sun-kissed skin. After we finished eating and attended to the kitten we were ready to head off to Vang Vieng, which was forty minutes away. As we started driving, I was in complete wonder. The high limestone karst formations, green mountains, Nam Song river, and surroundings looked like something out of the movie *Avatar*. Thai Bae had not described this place well enough when he said it was beautiful... it was spectacular!

Random animals were walking up and down the street next to the car. I'm talking cows and other large animals you would not expect to stroll up and down the streets in the western world. I was blinded to all of this the night before in the dark, so my breath was taken away at the sights. We finally arrived, and I realized that Vang Vieng is actually a tourist town with lots of caves, hiking, treks, and things to do along the river. It was amazing to me that I was in this place, way up in the mountains, in a country that I barely knew existed a few months ago. That thought hypnotized me as I excitedly began to think of how many other mountain villages, small towns, and jungle communities were tucked away in the world for me to explore — waiting for me to find them.

The next day, we decided to head back to Vientiane because Bruce got a business call and needed to get back to Thailand. Riding back in the morning was nothing like the scary ride there, when I'd thought I might end up just as dead as the night. I could witness all the beauty as we drove out of the mountains, and I had no choice but to scream "Wow!" every couple of minutes. Thai Bae felt vindicated with every excited sound leaving my mouth. His decision to convince us it was worth the trip was validated. I knew I needed to take it all in, because what were the chances I'd ever be here again? My brain absorbed every moment of the drive like it was the most special moment of my life. I thought how amazing it was that we got caught in the dark and had to sleep in an actual village, even though at the time I was pissed. But that's the thing about life; you have to trust in the timing, knowing there's a thread weaving everything together to create a beautiful piece of fabric. The journey includes every stitch you need. It was a reminder to stay open.

***

Finally, back in Vientiane, Thai Bae gave Bruce the keys and directions to drive back, saying he and I could catch a VIP Bus to Chiang Mai once we secured my visa. Bruce needed to get back ASAP, so off he went with Sawadee in tow. We needed to find a room, but it was high tourist season, which made it difficult—most places were booked. Vientiane is the capital and French-influenced from its colonial days, so the architecture was far from what we'd experienced up in the village or Vang Vieng. On our seventh try, we finally found a guesthouse that had an available room, and it happened to be in a prime location. We put our bags in the room and went to find food. A beautiful pizzeria was right around the corner, and my eyes got big like those of a kid who had just seen a unicorn. Pizza is my favorite food, and that was exactly what I needed.

"You always more happy about pizza than you are about me," Thai Bae said with a sarcastic laugh.

"I mean... it isssssss pizzzzzza," I joked to get under his skin while making my eyes big.

Knowing my sense of humor, he tried to imitate the laugh in my voice, which jumpstarted my actual laugh. Here we were, walking down the street, both laughing, mine an authentic laugh, his a daunting tease, towards a pizzeria that had jazz playing in Vientiane.

We both ordered our own six-cut pies and I had my favorite, pineapple juice, with it.

After we finished eating, we went to the local night market that lined the street with colorful booths, housing everything you could possibly imagine. The sounds of negotiations filled the air as everyone was trying to secure the lowest price they could. We found a spot and sat and talked by the river for a little bit, laughing and carrying on as we always did, then headed back to our guesthouse. The next day, we visited some more of the city on foot, and the farther away we got from the tourist path, the more looks I received. At one point, Thai Bae was so sick of people staring at me he put his arm around me, thinking I must be sick of it as well. I wasn't, and I barely noticed it at that point. He was much more irritated than me.

The day finally came for us to go to the embassy. I was nervous, knowing that if I didn't get approved for a three-month visa, it would mean I couldn't go back to Thailand. I had all my documents, pictures, and was ready to go. We got a tuk-tuk and made our way. To our surprise, even though we got there as soon as it opened, there was already a long line of people who had also been waiting over the long weekend. The line moved quickly, so it only took a couple of hours until I was able to hand in my paperwork. We were told to come back in the afternoon to pick up my visa, if approved.

While we waited, we headed to get lunch at a nearby restaurant that was packed. The waiter asked if an older white man could sit at our rather large table with us, and we both said, "Yes! Tell him to come over." Little did I know the synchronicity was about to be on eerie level 10. The man sat down, slightly uncomfortable, feeling like he was imposing. Thai Bae and I both started talking to him to let him know we were happy to have him, and he immediately loosened up. Ten minutes into our random conversation, we started getting to the good part.

"I've been working at various universities around the world for the past ten years and decided to take a six-month break. So I'm going to Thailand for the next two months or so once I get my visa," our new friend informed me after I asked his traveling story.

"I worked at a college back in the States for eight years," I responded, thinking that was kind of ironic.

Come to find out, this man's first job at the collegiate level was at the school I worked at. He had worked there for six years, way before I was there. Both our mouths dropped.

"What are the chances of meeting someone in Laos who actually used to work at the same exact place I worked at back in the States, and the waiter happened to seat us together?" I said, in complete shock, but he was clearly in more shock than I was.

"I don't even know what to say. This is beyond bizarrre!" he responded, still in awe. His face was in complete disbelief, and he kept looking at me with an "is this real life?" expression.

I began to tell him, "I call these touch moments. One of my favorite shows was called *Touch*, and the show reveals how we all are intertwined in miraculous ways. We have no idea how little 'coincidence' actually comes into play. It's like the East Asian Red String —"

"Red string of fate! I actually just read something about that," he interrupted, shaking his head with his jaw dropped. "Wow! I'm so glad we met. I was having a crappy day, but now I feel so much better," he finished.

I expected weird encounters like that. I was used to them, but was still tickled pink every time one happened. It was like the weekend while strolling through a local market, alone in Chiang Mai, a random older white man came up to me and started chatting away. Twenty minutes into the conversation, we figured out he was from the same town my dad grew up in. To put this in perspective, my dad grew up in a small town in Delaware that nobody has heard of. This man knew exactly where my grandmother's house was when I described it. So now in Laos, I was having yet another eerie touch moment to add to the books. We wrapped up eating and headed back to the embassy to finally ease all my fears and get my visa.

Waiting, waiting some more, and more... forty-five minutes seemed like four hours! My number was called to stand in line; I was anxious to get to the front. Finally, I was at the window with a short Thai lady looking at me, then down, then back up at me to make sure I was the same person in the passport photo. I was easy to recognize, being there was nobody else who looked like me among the white and Asian faces in the crowd. She signed a couple things, had me sign a couple things, then handed me my passport with my new visa attached. I was clear for the next three months! Two months straight, and then a quick visit to the consulate in Chiang Mai for an additional month.

"Yesssss!" I said as I start smiling from ear to ear with the weight of the world off my shoulders. This was a time I had not been balanced, aligned, or trusting. I had created three different scenarios that didn't end well, all with me not getting a visa...

Sometimes I witness myself playing out the worst-case scenarios over and over, rehearsing everything that can go wrong. There's nothing wrong with seeing things from all sides so you don't have any blind spots, but that's different from letting the things that could possibly go wrong steal your joy in the present moment. Thinking about what could go wrong over and over did nothing but make me an irritable bitch with a headache from my underlying anxiety. That anxiety came directly from not being in control, and there is no way I can always be in control, nor do I want to be. I wouldn't judge myself for it, only silently observe myself and leave it at that. I believe the simple act of making ourselves conscious of the things we do that are not benefiting us is the first step, and one of the most powerful acts we can engage in. Carl Jung once said, "Until you make the unconscious conscious it will rule your life and you will call it fate." Those triggers are always the things that let me know it's time to explore.

We were finally done and made our way back to the border after collecting our things from the guest house. I've crossed countries by air, car, and boats. My least favorite has to be on foot. The line was long, and it was hot. Thai nationals had a separate line from foreigners that moved much quicker, so Thai Bae was through his line an hour before I was. Luckily the man behind me was chatty — so we kept each other entertained. Finally making my way through the border control line, I was elated to be back in Thailand. We caught a tuk-tuk to the nearby bus station, and I was thankful there was a VIP bus heading back to Chiang Mai in the next couple of hours. Just enough time to sit down, eat, then get some snacks for the all-night ride.

We were on our way back to Thailand. Sitting in the window seat, I slept through most of the bus ride with my head on Thai Bae, smelling his oils, which calmed me even more than the peace I intuitively felt.

At the crack of dawn, with roosters going through their morning routine, we were back in Chiang Mai. A sense of relief came over me that made me question, *Maybe this IS home?*

14

IS THIS HOME?

Just another day around the way.

Feeling good today…

~Queen Latifah

My schedule was mapped out so that I only had coaching clients a couple days a week; they were usually extremely early in the morning, which would be evening in the States. This meant most of my days were free to do whatever I wanted. A lot of times, I did absolutely nothing and loved it. I would go to my favorite neighborhood places to get some fruit from my fruit man or a fresh coconut from my coconut lady and then pick a place to eat from the few I frequented regularly. Most of them knew what to give me as soon as I walked in the door, because I would eat the same things every single time. I filled my days working, reading, listening to podcasts and music, doing yoga, journaling, creating things, meditating, watching movies, but a lot of times, simply listening to the birds. For some reason those birds brought me so much peace. I'd be doing something, and then I'd hear them as they perched themselves on the window ledge. Thai Bae had put some bird food on it, so they loved stopping by regularly. I would try and figure out what they were saying and would then drift into nothingness. For the first time, maybe ever, I was able to just be.

I met all kind of interesting people as I was out and about. I met an Irish man in his late sixties who had once bicycled across Europe. This same man had come to the States and stayed illegally for ten years! He finally decided he should be responsible and turned himself in after those ten years, thinking he could properly obtain papers and was immediately sent to an immigration detention center for months. He said it was hell on earth; they thought he was an intelligence operative. I met an older widowed woman who decided to travel the world at seventy-five after her husband's death. Each person I met ignited a different part of me.

Going to the post office a couple times a week was one of the errands I ran for Thai Bae. Awaiting me at the counter was a stern older Thai man who had a permanent grimace seemingly tattooed on his face. Every single time I pulled a number from the dispenser to be waited on, I'd hope and pray to get the *other* guy, but for some reason, I always got Mr. Stern. I'd speak my best Thai with a huge smile, but he never came close to budging. It was a face-off I was starting to think I'd never win. A couple months into this challenge, my chance finally emerged to win him over.

An older Australian woman came into the post office while I was at the counter. She didn't know the procedures and was quite aggressive in a jolly way. In her confusion, she immediately came up front to ship her things without taking a number. Mr. Stern was trying to ask her what she was shipping, but she couldn't understand a word he was saying and vice versa. He looked at me, completely puzzled as she talked in English, and his eyes begged me to help.

Aha! I lit up, knowing my chance had finally presented itself! I interpreted what each of them was saying to the best of my ability, and I showed her the proper procedure. He said "Thank you" in English, and in our fifteen or more encounters, that was the first hint of a smile I had gotten. After that day, instead of his usual scowl, I was upgraded to a stern smirk. I was satisfied.

Thai Bae always wanted me to come to work with him, and sometimes I obliged. I would spend the day at one of the farms, sitting under a tree and staring at the sky for hours and hours or reading a book. The dozen or so Thai women doing various things with the fruit on the farm loved it when I came, even though I couldn't understand them and they couldn't understand me. Some of them brought their small children, and I spent some time teaching them English, and they attempted to teach me Thai, giggling when I messed up the tones, inflections, and words.

On some days, he and I would spend the day looking at farms he was considering buying. I spent a considerable amount of time in the heart of

Thailand. I don't mean hanging in pockets of the city that have been made into comfy areas for foreigners to feel at home... Those parts often reminded me of the gentrification that was taking place in my hometown of Pittsburgh, Pennsylvania. *I spent time in real Thailand.* I ate dinner in the mountains at the humble houses of some of the women who worked on Thai Bae's farms. Somehow one morning I found myself sitting behind a juice stand with a local family in the mountains. Another day a woman whose family owned one of the farms he was renting for the season told me to come with her in Thai. At that point I could understand some Thai but still couldn't speak it well.

I looked at Thai Bae, and he said, "It okay. She want you to go to her house. I be done in couple hours come get you."

He was extremely protective of me, so I knew if he said it was okay, it was okay. I hopped on the back of her motorbike, and off we went. I spent the next couple of hours with her and her two teenage daughters, one of whom was learning English in school. We laughed, tried to talk, danced around, and basically played charades to communicate. Here I was in Thailand, thousands of miles away from home, sharing moments with strangers I could not have dreamed up. Literally.

I cherished those moments in random strangers' homes, in towns I would have never known existed, knowing only synchronicity could have brought me to so many authentic experiences in a foreign place. These experiences have become a part of my DNA. The genuine curiosity, warmth, and love they naturally exuded came through. Everyone was always trying to feed me or share whatever they had.

When I decided my intentions for the trip, my soul obviously made a contract and conspired with the universe to have me spend an extended amount of time in a country where the people are naturally *curious, happy, and free*. They knew how to stay in the moment, embracing the blessing of seeing a sunset, honoring and appreciating the old man next door and his wisdom, laughing with their friends and family, eating good food, and smiling for no visible reason. It was easy. They were content with who they were, not attaching their worth to what they had, what they did, or what people thought of them. Everyone was treated with respect and greeted with a warm smile in these small mountain villages.

I've learned and evolved into taking nothing personally. Knowing this allowed me to embrace random strangers having tons of questions, wanting to touch my hair, touch my face, or asking what might have been offensive questions. The world is a big place, but all roads lead somewhere, as someone close to me always says. What I knew for sure was every road and breadcrumb I had followed led me to experiences I couldn't have dreamed of. My internal GPS knew exactly where I needed to be. So I embraced the curiosity of these people surrounding the black American girl with hair like a lion and eyes like a rare tiger — knowing I'd leave them with a little black girl magic as a thank-you for reminding me what life is all about.

***

Meditating with a former monk, which Thai Bae is, was hilarious. Sometimes we visited a beautiful temple that had a hidden waterfall. He could sit, not moving an inch, for hours. A butterfly could land on his nose, and he would be so far gone it wouldn't make a difference. My limit was thirty to forty-five minutes without moving, so I'd quietly get up and watch to see if he flinched. He knew I might escape into the trees and trails, so somehow the only thing that would get him to shift his energy was when I started tip-toeing off into the nearby forest for an adventure.

He'd say, "I feel you — don't go far, pwease!"

I'd giggle and escape into the forest...

Then there was Thai Bae's small temple, one of my absolute favorite places in Thailand, tucked up in the mountains, a forty-minute drive from the city, way off-road. Meditation platforms, hammocks, mountains close and in the distance, streams, rice fields, and enchanting paths all made this place magical, like something from a postcard or movie. It was serene, both in sight and feeling, a place I could stay for hours. We would walk around the grounds after chatting with the monk, in Thai of course, who was one of his good friends. Sometimes the monk would go for a three-week walk. During these walks, monks engage in walking meditations and embrace the silence. They receive and live off alms, food offerings from the lay people. I found it all fascinating getting first-hand accounts of the things I had read in books.

There were a few stray dogs on the land that always hung around the temple; the monk and groundskeepers fed them regularly. But when the dogs saw Thai Bae, and eventually me, entering, they greeted us with such excitement, chasing us everywhere we went for hours. We walked the paths around the temple grounds, sometimes for hours, running into random cows at times. Being around each other was easy, and we had fun doing nothing but walking and talking, or just being silent without awkwardness.

One day we went to a festival at a bigger temple deep in the mountains; one of the farm real estate agents had invited us to it. This agent loved when I came around and always told Thai Bae to translate that he "had no idea American girls looked like that; I will move to America!" I just laughed.

When we entered the festival, all eyes were on us, in particular me. I stuck out like a sore thumb. Keep in mind this is in the mountains, not the city, and most of these people probably had never seen a black person in person. Everyone started bringing me things and surrounding me. It was overwhelming to say the least, because it was an actual crowd. The crowd buzzed, and I couldn't understand a word anyone was saying, so I just smiled, letting them all touch me as much as they wanted. Thai Bae kept looking at me to make sure I was okay, then I finally squeezed his hand, letting him know I had had enough. He said some things in Thai to the crowd, and a woman pulled us to go sit back away from the people. I'm an outgoing introvert, so if you meet me in person, you'd assume I'm 100% extrovert. But I really prefer to be alone most of the time. After an hour of being stared at by a hundred-plus people nonstop, I was exhausted. This was why I much preferred his tiny temple where everyone was used to seeing me.

***

One of the things Thai Bae and I had in common was our love for movies. I love movies, all kinds, but I can watch just about any thriller, suspense, action, or sci-fi. Living in another country allowed me to grasp some of the normal things that I wouldn't have experienced on a vacation. Going to the post office, grocery shopping, mechanic shop, and movies become experiences in themselves when you notice how similar but vastly different a place is from your home. My first movie in Thailand was *Spectre 007*. I was extremely excited to go to the movies since I hadn't been in months, traveling around. Little did I know I was about to have a next-level movie experience when Thai Bae handed me my ticket that he'd purchased from the electronic kiosk, and it said 4DX.

"What the heck is 4D?" I asked, perplexed.

"Ohhhh, you never see 4D movie? Ha-ha-ha, I pop you 4D cherry! Just wait, you will love," he said while beaming from ear to ear in anticipation.

We walked into the cinema and to our designated numbered seats smack in the middle of the hall with our 3D glasses and goodies in hand. I sat down in the plush and comfortable red seats, looking around to see if I could identify what was different about 4DX, but there were no clues. The Thai commercials and movie trailers began, and I became completely annoyed, noticing every Thai person on the screen was damn near white. The people I had seen around in town and up in the mountains were melanated from light to a rich chocolate color. This was not represented on the screen at all. I noticed the same thing when looking at beauty products in the stores. Everyone was almost white in the advertisements. One of the reasons I wanted to visit Thailand specifically was because it was the only Asian country that has never been colonized by Europeans. Still somehow the European standard for beauty seeped in, and lighter skin is praised. Meanwhile, the Thai people with darker skin are some of the most gorgeous of all Thai people. After being in the sun for any amount of time, Thai Bae became copper brown. That, actually, was when I found him the most attractive.

All of a sudden everyone in the theater stood up. I looked around as he said to me, "Stand for King."

Majestic, heavenly, stadium-sounding music with the assistance of a choir that sounded like only the best voices in the world were chosen to participate started overtaking the room. It was the Thai national anthem with an accompanying video featuring the King. King Bhumibol has since passed, but he was at the time the longest reigning monarch in the world. The Thai people show extreme regard for him and their anthem, and if you don't stand up, someone will politely inform you to do so. The video playing along with the music almost brought tears to my eyes. Not because it was particularly touching, but the musical build-up at the end was overwhelmingly majestic in surround sound—the same feeling you get from a really powerful church choir. I didn't have a clue what they were saying, but the sound ran through my body and gave me chills.

We all sat down, and the movie began. I was not prepared for 4DX. I screamed, "Wooooah" as my chair shook and jerked with the fast-paced car chases. At one point I felt a mist of water, then wind, sometimes fog... It was amazing, like 3D on overload. I thought to myself how cool it was that I could be in the mountains with limited technology, basically going back 100 years, then right back in the city, forty minutes later, experiencing technology at its finest. The juxtaposition was what made Chiang Mai such an enchanting place. Well, that, and the $400 rent for a fully furnished modern apartment.

15

AM I GOING TO DIE?

As my reflection of light I'mma lead you, and
whatever's right, I'mma feed you.

~Common

It was a beautiful Sunday around 11:00 a.m., and I had been put in charge of sister-sitting Bruce's eighteen-year-old sister, who was visiting before she went back home to China. Thai Bae and Bruce had gone to southern Thailand to check out some farms, so she would be alone for the day, and Bruce volunteered me to look after her. I approached the corner where we had decided to meet and immediately saw her long, silky black hair bouncing around her face as she waved and jumped to get my attention. She knew it was me from pictures, and because I was well... black. She looked at me, smiling, and said, "Woah, pretty!!" as I laughed. She spoke maybe fifty words of English, so we immediately began playing charades in between those few words she knew. Her easy-going personality was filled with an innocence I remembered once having. She was full of light, and it made me smile on the inside. One thing that is common around the world is love for food, and neither of us had eaten. I knew her brother loved noodles, so I took her to a place I knew that served noodles he loved. It was a hit! She surrendered to the amazing mix of flavors, doing a happy dance when she took each bite

Girls all over the world love shopping, so next we headed to a bunch of local boutiques where she could grab some things to take home. We were having a great time together and decided to get $5 massages after shopping before heading to the Sunday Night Market, called the Sunday Walking Street.

This street market was something I frequented religiously, often just to get food from a few of my favorite vendors who made amazing fruits smoothies, the best satay, and these dessert things that tasted like donuts, but better. Sunday was always the day I'd feed my face until I couldn't eat anymore. The food is always inexpensive in Thailand, but at the Sunday Night Walking Street, it's dirt cheap.

An entire street is shut down for blocks, and there are booths and tables of food, clothing, jewelry, and anything else you can think of calling out your name as you take the crowded march. My favorite vendors were outside the less crowded temple, so we made our way there. They had switched the setup from what I was used to at my favorite booth, and I pointed out what I thought was a plate full of *chicken* satay. Since I was feeling particularly hungry that day from all the walking around, I decided I was going all in, getting two plates. The juicy chicken was grilled to perfection, and the accompanying peanut dipping sauce that comes with chicken satay was blended perfectly, just like it was every week. We went around to a few more booths so Bruce's sister could try all the food she wanted as well. We had spent a full eight hours out and about, so at that point, she was holding my hand everywhere we went, not wanting to get mixed into the crowd. It was endearing how comfortable she had gotten with me. We were drained and had had enough after our full day of adventures.

Exhausted after putting baby sister in a cab with a driver I knew to make sure she got back to Bruce's place safely, I ran home because my stomach was absolutely killing me. It started to twist and turn as if it were a gymnast doing backflips. Five minutes later, I thought an animal had entered the room when I heard my stomach making a funny noise. Before I knew it, I was running to the bathroom and to the toilet bowl, where I began throwing up everything. As soon as I thought there was no way anything else could come up, I'd explode into a violent episode, projecting even more. It went on for hours. I couldn't drink water without it coming up or out the other end. It was gross, and I felt like crap.

Thai Bae was far away, and I just wanted to sleep to escape from this misery. When he called to check on me, I put on my best efforts to act fine because I knew he'd get on the next flight and come back if I told him anything was wrong. Since he had begged me to come with them, he'd also feel justified in believing I should go everywhere with him. I felt completely alone and homesick. All of a sudden, Thailand didn't quite feel like home, and I just wanted to be back in the States.

Days had gone by, and I was still sick — not quite as violently, but still sick. *Should I go to the hospital? Did I contract some rare disease that makes people unable to eat?* At one point, I actually thought to myself that I might die in Thailand, half believing it and half knowing I can be dramatic. I had no clue what was going on; all I knew was I couldn't keep food down. I thought it was most likely food poisoning, so I made sure to keep drinking fresh coconuts from a half block down the street and chicken broth. This way I knew I was at least getting some nutrition before it came back up or out. I didn't tell anyone back home how sick I was, knowing they would panic. Then I finally start feeling a little better, right in time for Thai Bae to return for the Sunday market the following week. My appetite was back, and I was finally holding food down. We went to the market and I pointed to the "chicken satay." He immediately began speaking forcibly in Thai to the man behind the stand who switched out my order.

"You pick pork!" he said to me, knowing I don't eat pork and hadn't for decades.

A spotlight came on in my head and a gameshow host appeared telling me I had finally solved the puzzle; the reason I had been sick was because I ate two plates of pork the previous week. The chicken and pork look so much alike, and I hadn't paid enough attention. There was no way I was ever making that mistake again.

I had been wanting to go vegan for a couple years for various reasons, including animal cruelty, the negative impact of animal agriculture on the environment, and my health. The universe got my attention and this was the push I needed to jumpstart that transition. I decided I would start practicing my values of love, compassion, and responsibility when I made a conscious choice what to fuel my personal temple three times a day. My journey to becoming a plant-based vegan started right there in Chiang Mai, Thailand, where so many other things had evolved within me... I was following the breadcrumbs, and this one was clear as day.

16

THAI FRIENDS

I live for the nights I can't remember with the
people I won't forget. Spending all the money
I worked my ass off,
for the things I won't regret.

~Drake

Thai Bae's friends became my friends. Their
English ranged between five percent to seventy
percent, but it didn't matter, they were MY people. If
they didn't see me for a couple days, they'd want to
know where I'd been. His neighbor, Anh, became my
gay husband. Somehow, he knew just about every
state in the USA, and when we walked anywhere and
saw a foreigner, he would start up a quick chat with
them and add that I was Miss Illinois. The next day
I'd be Miss California, then Miss Texas. He got a kick

out of seeing everyone's reactions. After the tenth time, realizing he was never going to stop, I started playing along with him.

Whenever I'd see him, if I had on a tight shirt, he would grab my boobs and squirm, "Soooo nice sooo nice and squishy!" I'd smack his hands, and he'd flip his nonexistent fake hair. We'd both laugh.

When Thai Bae was sitting down, if I walked up, Anh would get behind him and start making sexy gestures towards him without him knowing, trying to provoke me. I would die laughing, and Thai Bae would want to know what I was laughing about.

One of my favorite nights with Anh was when he was hosting a drag pageant and show. I tagged along, having no idea what to expect. Let me tell you, I have never seen so much fabulousness in my entire life! These gals were dressed to a T, makeup on serve, and "Yesssssssss weeerrrrrkkkk" was coming out of my mouth left and right, especially when three of them were doing an impersonation of Beyoncé's "Single Ladies." It was a full-on pageant of epic-ness.

Anh was absolutely hilarious, fabulous, and always put a smile on my face.

Then there was Thai Bae's gorgeous, fiery best girlfriend whom he called his sister. She was obsessed with trying to get me to hang out and party with her.

"We go out tonight, you come. He stay. Okay?" she tried over and over again.

The only other foreigner in the crew was Brenden from New Zealand. He was thirty-nine-ish, and when the seven of the Thai crew started talking in Thai nonstop, we were happy to have each other to communicate with. One day we went way outside of the city to get some lanterns in bulk for the upcoming festival. The owner of the small shop made such a big deal over Brenden and me, we had to take pictures for ten minutes with her and her family. Thai Bae just laughed and laughed as Brenden and I nervously looked at each other, wondering when it was going to stop.

But my birthday was the day they surprised me. Before Thai Bae swept me up into the mountains for an evening of massages, a restaurant with an amazing view, and a visit to another secret temple — they had cake and a gift waiting for me. It was comical and endearing, hearing them sing happy birthday in English with their strong accents. The entire time they were singing, I thought to myself, *Never forget this; this is hilarious.*

***

One night, ten of us were all hanging outside around midnight with a table full of food and drinks when all of a sudden a black guy rode past on a bike. Thai Bae hopped up with such excitement, running into the middle of the street, chasing the bike down screaming, "Hey Bwack guy, Bwack guy! My girlfriend Bwack and wants to talk to Bwack people! Come back, come back, pweeaasse."

I was mortified and laughing at the same time, in disbelief that he was chasing this poor guy down. I always talked about missing black people, and he saw an opportunity and was determined to fix it. Boy, did this man love me, and he was going to make sure he didn't let the black guy get away.

The bike immediately turned around in what appeared like slow motion for me, and behold, it was Marvin from New York. I immediately could tell from his swag he was my kind of people.

"There was no way I could resist seeing who was screaming 'black guy, my girlfriend's black,'" Marvin said, shaking his head and laughing at the same time.

I apologized for Thai Bae's screaming at him down the street in the middle of the night, but he thought it was hilarious. We still crack up laughing about that to this day, and it was the night he ended up eating a live insect after hanging out with us for a couple of hours.

***

It wasn't long before I learned I was dealing with the real life Dr. Dolittle. We were dragging a different animal to the vet every week, no exaggeration. One evening I was waiting for him to pick me up for dinner when the phone rang. "Come outside, I have night bird in car and must take to vet."

Here we go again, I thought while rolling my eyes. This was cute and charming the first four or five animals, but it was getting ridiculous. I got downstairs as he rolled down the window. I reluctantly looked inside only to find it was a freaking owl sitting on his leg, just chilling.

"Dude, that is an owl!" I screamed in disbelief.

"Yes. Bird of the night. That what I say. Get in, we take to hospital then go eat." He tried to assure me, making it seem simple and easy.

With much hesitation, I opened the door, and the owl, most likely sensing my nervous energy, went from calmly sitting on his knee to flying around in the car.

"You have to calm down, you scare he," Thai Bae said to me.

"It's a wild owl, dude. How about you come back and get me after?" I asserted.

He calmed the owl down, setting him on the floor in the back of the car. Good thing it was his beat-up car, because I probably was making the poor thing poop all over the place. As we were driving, he smiled from ear to ear as I was tense, sitting as still as I possibly could, alert, waiting to get smacked in the head any second by this owl chilling in the backseat like his homie. When we finally arrived at the vet, I got out of the car as quickly as humanly possible. As we walked into the vet's office, the entire staff laughed because at this point, they thought it was funny he brought in different animals so often. Mind you, this was NOT free. As they exchanged a bunch of words in Thai, I could tell the conversation was not going the way he planned; I could see it in their faces, gestures, and the few words I could make out.

He turned around waving me to come while saying, "Pa!" I looked at the staff. They were still laughing, smiling, and giving me the look.

"Why do you still have the owl?" I asked.

"They no take this kind of bird to fix," he said as if it weren't a problem.

"Soooo, what are you going to do?" I questioned, seriously wondering what was going to happen next.

"I make he better myself!" He informed me like I should have known.

"What? Oh, hell no," I asserted, knowing good and well I had to put my foot down, or he'd have me taking care of all kinds of animals sooner than later.

"Come on, come on. I get cage. It be fine in a week. No problem," he pleaded.

Long story short, he bought a cage and found a friend up in the mountains to keep the owl. He went by every day, "nursing the owl back to health," which somehow... he did. Nursing things back to life was his specialty.

17

TROUBLE IN PARADISE

Burn a stoge and let her know, sweetheart I got to have it. She telling me commitment is something she can't manage. Wake up the next morning she was gone like it was magic.

~Yasiin Bey aka The Mighty Mos Def

Every relationship and friendship has *a price of admission:* Something the other person does that irritates you but you are willing to put up with because it's worth having them in your life. It is our job to know what our own non-negotiable things are, which are the things that we could never pay or accept as a price of admission.

Thai Bae wanted to get married, for me to become a Thai citizen, to move to Thailand permanently and have a baby. He started talking about it continuously to the point it started causing crazy tension. Marriage wasn't high on my priority list at that point, and after only four or five months, was not something I was ready to jump into. If I do get married, it will NOT be a normal marriage. I'm likely to get married and not tell anyone. It's something my husband and I will design specifically for our individual and mutual mental, emotional, spiritual, and physical needs, wants, growth, autonomous paths, and intertwined paths. We will be real-life partners. That works only when both parties are in a relationship for growth, partnership, and true connection.

There's a beauty in being able to compromise without compromising one's self; Thai Bae wanted me to compromise myself. I don't want to be in a relationship to combat my or another person's insecurities. I want to be in a relationship because it makes me a better person and also makes my partner a better person. He wanted to get married to ensure he didn't lose me. I have a securely attached personality in relationships; I didn't need to know where he was every moment, and if I didn't talk to him a million times, it wasn't a problem. Then something happened that made me question things.

It was a beautiful night and we were getting back from a tasty dinner. I was especially excited because we had just gone to the movies to see the new Star Wars movie in 4DX, again. As we entered his place I was laughing remembering a funny thing that happened to me earlier that day.

"Oh I forgot to tell you the funniest thing…" I said through my laughter.

I was reaching for my hairbrush that he often said looked like a brush you're supposed to clean shoes with.

"Stop laughing tell the story," he said rolling his eyes and smiling.

He always complained that I find my own stories so funny I laugh so hard while talking he can't understand me.

I continued, "So… I was walking and this Thai man with long hair, a fake you, came up to me. He could hardly speak English. I didn't know what he was trying to say or tell me. Then he finally said 'you me go eat.' It was the cutest thing ever!"

I was now brushing my hair and waiting for him to laugh along with me, thinking he would find it hilarious. Instead, he came over and began kissing me. Ten seconds later he was down to my neck and I felt a feeling I had not felt in decades, and had only felt once before in my life. He was giving me a hickey also known as a sucker-bite! One thing I'm not is a sucker.

I took my thumb and pressed it into the center of his throat the way my stepdad taught me years ago. I knew that would get him off of me immediately as I screamed, "What are you doing?!"

The hairbrush was still in my hand and it was taking everything in me not to bash his face with it. He stood proudly admiring the new artwork he had just branded me with, and that was his intention. I grabbed my purse and swiftly left; I didn't want to end up in Thai jail. Know thine own weaknesses and govern accordingly. This was a problem.

There's a fine line between being protective and being possessive. I don't want to be possessed and have no desire to possess another human being. He became possessive. Another time we were riding his bike, and a truck almost hit us as we were pulling to a red light. This normally peaceful, happy-go-lucky man I had grown to love was now screaming at the top of his lungs in Thai, trying to get off his bike as I'm sitting on the back, trying to hold him down and calm him.

He kept saying, "I not calm down; he could kill you. I beat he ass!"

He was trying to get off the bike to drag this man out of the vehicle in the middle of traffic. I was in complete disbelief at his temper. The light turned green, and the terrified young man drove off.

He kept telling everyone we were getting married and going to have a baby. I became more annoyed every time it left his lips. I was starting to feel like the walls were closing in on me.

The multiple things about him that drove me mad were prices of admission I was possibly willing to pay. He was impulsive to the point of bordering on irresponsible at times. He had a temper that made me have to count to ten and breathe so I wouldn't react. He had no understanding of the black experience in America and could be insensitive, and he was hyper-insecure, thinking I was going to leave him for a "bwack guy with big bwack dick" (his words, not mine). Those were things that I *might* have been able to deal with.

There's something about never having to question how a person feels about you, their word, and their intentions, that creates a space for deep intimacy — and we had that for sure, but that wasn't enough.

The price of admission I wasn't willing to pay was him constantly trying to convince me into getting married, moving to Thailand permanently, and having a baby in the next year. I know my price of admission doesn't include a baby or babies, and that was something I could see he yearned for. I didn't want him to give up being a father, knowing I could never replace — and wouldn't want to — the longing he had. I knew he'd be an awesome dad, and that's something he should experience. It just isn't something I want.

And here lies one of the biggest problems in my eyes that our society has placed on a relationship: we deem it a failure if it doesn't end with someone dying. Till death do us part, or else you've failed. We aren't able to acknowledge that something can be beautiful and serve its purpose for a period of time, then end, without it being a failed relationship.

We don't give ourselves permission to change our minds.

We don't give ourselves permission to evolve.

Sometimes we can't see the beauty in clarity that can only come through experience.

It can be beautiful seeing how a relationship is not a good fit but still being able to acknowledge its significance in your life for the portion of time it served you. Sometimes we lack the ability to witness someone being beautifully human without wanting to cling with an attachment that is fear-based. I was now able to recognize when I had an experience in its totality, knowing its purpose had been served. It was okay to move on. It was okay to set someone free. And it didn't mean something tragically bad had to happen. It meant I loved myself and him enough to know that it would not serve either of us in the future. I had made that mistake, not ending my relationship with Kamau five years in when I should have, continuing it far past the expiration date. I wasn't going to make that mistake again, so I asked the universe to give me clarity.

***

Breadcrumbs

A good friend of mine whom I dated back in high school and college days, whom I hadn't talked to in almost a year, texted me out of the blue, "*Pray Love Eat* is over; get your ass home. It's time!" He totally messed up the name of the book, so I cracked up laughing as I read it.

I replied, "Yo! You aren't the boss of me. Don't tell me what to do unless you're buying me a ticket."

Literally an hour later I had a ticket from him in my email inbox, back to the USA, leaving in four days. I was in complete shock with mixed emotions. I couldn't believe it. He actually bought me a ticket home because he had a feeling? I had planned on going back to Laos for another visa extension that weekend, but now I was going home? It was one of those signs I never ignore—a breadcrumb.

The funny thing was, my grandmother's brother, my Uncle Powell, who is basically like my grandfather, had just told my mother a few days before that it was time for me to "get my ass home." My dad ended up telling me that my overprotective cousin Dusty had asked him when I was coming home. "Enough was enough."

Then I found out the next day, my mom was going to be having her first major surgery ever, almost as soon as I got home. It was one of those surreal moments you know the universe aligned perfectly just for you. There was no way my friend could have known when he impulsively bought me a ticket that my mom would have to have surgery. But he had a feeling it was time for me to come home, so he bought me a ticket following his gut. There was no contemplation on my part; it was done.

***

I had repeatedly told Thai Bae I did not want to have a baby or get married so quickly. He continued to pressure me. I didn't have the courage to break up with him, because I still wasn't quite sure if I'd return or not. It all happened so fast and unexpectedly. So I told him I needed time to think once I got home.

We had my favorite meal before heading to the airport. He knew as he was driving me — in a somber mood, visibly agitated — that when I boarded that airplane, he would not share the same physical space or look me in the eyes ever again.

After checking in, he walked me to security as far as he could go. This was it. He looked deep in my eyes and said, "I know you will not come back. I love you." His eyes were completely filled with water, but a tear never dropped, as if he was hanging onto a little bit of hope. The moment he said those words... I knew they were true.

18

RETURNING THE GOLDEN BUDDHA

In my eyes, you see power and perfection. A
disguised flower with a warrior's reflection…

~Shawna Sharee

I was finally on the plane heading back home,
overlooking the land of smiles that helped lead me
back to myself, and I was reminded of the Golden
Buddha story.

In 1957, a monastery in Thailand was being
relocated. A giant clay Buddha was being moved
carefully by a group of monks. As they were moving
it, one of the monks noticed a crack in the clay with
something shiny gleaming through. Not wanting to
destroy the important Buddha, the monks decided to
take a break and call it a night. Curious and

protective, one of the monks went to check on the statue. While shining a light towards the Buddha, he noticed a reflection that really piqued his curiosity, so with a hammer and a chisel, he began chipping and chipping piece after piece of clay. Every piece revealed a brighter and brighter surface until the entire Buddha was no longer covered in clay. It was actually solid gold hiding beneath the surface!

It is thought that hundreds of years ago, when the monks were being attacked by the Burmese, they were clever and covered the Buddha in clay to protect it. All of the monks died, so there was no record that this clay Buddha was actually solid gold underneath all the protection.

This was symbolic of my journey. Every country, city, encounter, uncomfortable situation, smile, conversation, adventure, kiss, connection, laugh, bus ride, street, sunset, and moment in perfect solitude had chipped away pieces of clay, leading me back to my true, solid gold self. I had deep dived into my subconscious. My feet were dirty from the path I had walked along across six countries, and I shed many ways of thinking and being that no longer served me along the way. Although my feet were soiled, I was shining like the golden Buddha, not returning the same person I was when I left.

I was returning me.

19

7 THINGS I LEARNED

I met a gypsy and she hipped me to some life game. To stimulate then activate the left and right brain.

~Andre 3000

As I wrote this memoir, I reflected on the lessons I learned during the first of my travel journeys. They boil down to these seven things I hope you walk away with.

1. I gave myself permission to change my mind and get off autopilot.

We are born pure, but from the moment we are born, we are programmed by those around us and society. Because of that programming, we move further and further away from our perfect whole selves. We are like sponges absorbing everything we see, hear, feel, and experience. We sense and notice our caretakers' reactions and emotions. We observe what we are praised for, rejected for, as well as what gets our needs met. *It is survival.* Automatically we create an imprint to do those things that make us feel accepted and loved. We learn how life seems to work, and before we know it, we have subconscious beliefs that dictate what we do, how we behave, and tell us what our life should look like. We start behaving as a computer program.

It wasn't until I started exploring my subconscious beliefs that I even realized I was operating on auto-pilot. I've always been a rebel, but the more I stopped clinging onto the expectations that I subconsciously created, the more I unveiled what my soul desired. I began exploring my limited beliefs, my triggers, my pain, and where I take the easy road to avoid things. These were all breadcrumbs that led me to my first awareness of being on autopilot — and taking control of the wheel.

There were so many times I witnessed myself staying in jobs, relationships, cities, hobbies, belief systems, etc., etc. that no longer served me, simply because quitting *seemed like failure* to my past programming. But once I gave myself permission to change my mind, I chose to see the beauty in things for what they were, even when they were not meant to follow me into my future.

So if something doesn't serve me, even if it once had, why would it be a bad thing to change my mind? I'm not advocating being irresponsible but instead staying curious. Remaining curious eventually provides clarity. What chases a truly curious mind? Evolution. And evolution involves *change*.

Keep refining through every experience. Let inner peace be your barometer for success.

2. I am enough.

We live in a culture that places so much value on how close to perfection we *seem.* But ironically, when I stopped striving for perfection, I could finally acknowledge and appreciate *all* that I am. The grit has just as much value as the sparkle.

When I start embracing my complete self I came to the realization that I am enough — flaws and all. By fully identifying, owning, healing, and integrating the parts of me that lived in the shadows, I was released from their cages. The freedom I craved was within me the entire time — I just wasn't accessing it because in essence, I was judging and rejecting myself.

Subconsciously reprogramming myself to know I am enough allows me to authentically show up as a whole person in every situation. Not because of anything I do, what I have, what I can give, what I say, what checkmarks I check off of the invisible list, or what mold I fit into, but because I was born enough. I was born whole. I was born worthy — and it is my birthright to show up in the world just as I am.

Audre Lorde once said, "Nothing I accept about myself can be used against me to diminish me."

Self-love is acceptance.

3. Being positive all the time is bullshit.

The pop fad of "thinking positive," in the way it has been presented and interpreted, is sometimes a way to bypass real issues. I learned there's a way to reframe a situation so I am not dwelling on the negative aspects but instead inviting myself into a conversation. With a wider perspective I watch and address what triggers me, what is showing up in my life, and how I'm feeling. Then I can zoom in and look at these things as breadcrumbs for me follow and explore.

Triggers reveal the places inside of us where pain is slyly hiding. Ancient dormant pain that is begging to be seen can't be positively thought away. It will only mask in the safe spaces the ego provides. I choose to let my pain spill out, even when it makes me uncomfortable, so healing can take place.

Putting the pressure on myself to always stay positive limited my ability to truly become aware of and appreciate what was really going on inside of me. In the past I hadn't honored the act of simple awareness, without judgement, because I was in a competition with myself to "stay positive."

We find ourselves in situations that will either force us to evolve or stay trapped in a limited reality where we just recycle experiences, sometimes with different people or situations. Even though recycling felt safe, I was ready for evolution, so I was ready to get dirty if that's what it took. I asked myself, *What is here for me to learn about myself in this situation? Why is this happening? What is this reminding me of in my past? What am I missing? What is my subconscious programming that has gotten me here? Who am I being? What can I do differently? What do I need to make sure I'm okay in this moment?* These are the type of questions that allowed me to tap into the parts of me that needed healing.

Thinking positive is great, as long as you are not using it as a way to escape and run away from the darkness that you may need to explore. Ironically, sometimes exploring in the dark is the only way into the light.

4. I am responsible for my interpretation and energy.

It's so easy to get attached to our own perspective and ego, allowing very little room for the experiences of others. I believe that everyone is doing the best they can with their current level of consciousness. So when an Asian stranger touches my hair, I don't become offended. I choose to recognize they mean no harm and probably have not been exposed to black culture, where it is a big no-no to touch a black girl's hair without permission. Most likely, they are just excited and curious from a pure place. When I didn't want strangers' hands on my face, I'd simply smile and say "no" in a polite way, but never did I take offense unless I felt threatened or violated.

Same rule applies to personal relationships. The more you don't take personally, no matter what is done to you, the more space you create for your own happiness. This doesn't mean you aren't free to create boundaries when something or someone is toxic — it means you don't dwell on how wrong you were done. Everyone has issues, and people do things based on their own subconscious programming and sometimes pain. Let others process life and get the lessons and experiences they need *without you becoming collateral damage*.

I am responsible for my energy. I am responsible for how I show up in the world. I am responsible for my reactions. I am responsible for how I interpret the things that happen. I am responsible for creating healthy boundaries when boundaries are needed. These are all things I am in control of.

I figured out that if I look for reasons to be offended, I will always find them. Since everything I perceive is based on my own interpretation, I am responsible to check myself by gauging how my interpretations may be tainted by my past experiences, assumptions, and beliefs. This approach alone can allow you to show up in your life in a way that allows you to deeply connect with yourself and others.

There is massive freedom in self-accountability.

5. I changed my relationship with fear.

Fear is seen as some big bad thing. But, would you really want to be in the world without having any fear? Fear is an evolutionary component that developed to keep us alive and safe. Back in the day, we saw a lion and knew it was time to get far away. When I had the epiphany that fear is on my side, I start looking at it as an overprotective big brother. That shift in perspective changed my relationship with fear entirely.

I now realize fear shows up when he thinks I'm in danger or things are unknown, just doing his job based on real threats or past programming. It's an opportunity for me to see if my big brother is doing a good job protecting me or simply being over-protective, like he sometimes is. But if I see fear as the enemy, how can I make accurate assessments? How can I have a healthy conversation? How can I see my blind spots? Fear leaves breadcrumbs to point out things for me to explore internally.

There are many times I know my fear has kept me alive. So I'm not striving to not experience fear; I am aiming to have a healthy relationship with him. I can react to fear on autopilot or choose to investigate his concerns when he bring something to my attention.

Experiencing fear is not the same as giving into fear.

6. I became extremely intentional

An intention is an aim, purpose, or plan. When you operate with extreme intention in everything you do, you show up in the world with purpose, knowing what you want. About ten years ago in my earlier years as a college counselor, I came to the understanding that everything we do has a why behind it. No matter if we set an intention or not, we are always planting seeds that will eventually blossom. Setting an intention in as many moments as possible, allows us to choose what seed we are planting, and what type of harvest we reap.

For the past decade, I introduced living with intention into my life, but while in Hawaii I made the intentional decision to live with extreme intention. This meant deciding the why in as many moments, responses, conversations, actions, and thoughts as possible. There are three simple questions you can ask yourself at every moment: Why am I doing this? What is my intention behind this? What seed am I planting?

By intentionally directing your attention to these questions, you are activating your subconscious and conscious mind to work together. It's actually science. There is a part of our brains called the reticular activating system that scans through all the information we receive and decides to bring our attention to the things we've told it is important. By simply becoming more aware and conscious you will start to direct your brain to work in your favor.

Live with more intention, and you will undoubtedly plant the seeds that blossom into your wildest dreams.

7. Be open and surrender to magic and joy.

I'm now open to things being way better than I ever imagined. I stopped putting God in a box a long time ago, but now I expect the most mind-blowing coincidences, big and small. I expect miracles and I'm no longer afraid of abundance. I'm not afraid of joy or lasting happiness. I'm not afraid of taking chances. I'm not afraid of saying no, because I know what I desire is awaiting me in divine timing.

Why? Because I'm no longer waiting for the other shoe to drop. I'm shaking off my beliefs that having too much happiness or abundance is taking away from someone else. I'm leaving behind the belief that struggle is noble. We are all meant to live with miracles chasing us and there is enough in the world for us all to live out our purpose, abundantly.

I have a resilience that some question, thinking I live with my head in the clouds, but that's because I expect and trust the universe to show up — no matter how bad it gets or seems. I expect and know I'm worthy of magic. I do my part to the best of my ability, and I expect to be met halfway. I expect the trail of breadcrumbs to either lead me to what's holding me back so I can deal with it, or light the path for me to follow...

Make sure you are open to things being way better than you planned. Welcome goodness when it shows up no matter how far out of your comfort zone it feels; melt and exhale into it.

Conclusion

Traveling the world the way I do may not be your thing, but there is probably something deep within you that you desire and dream of. I hope you take my story and these seven *aha!* moments as a blueprint to explore and follow your own breadcrumbs.

Know that what you desire is possible, start making a plan, trust in the process, and open the door for magic to flow in. Sit still. Do things without telling the world — just for the bliss in it. When those times come along that you can't make sense of what's happening, remember that feeling of énouement I felt so often — the bitter-sweetness of arriving in the future unable to tell my past self how it turns out. Your future self wants you to enjoy your *entire* journey. Allow yourself to experience every feeling, fear, desire, and moment, knowing that if you intentionally show up for your life, everything will work out, and work out even more amazing than you ever anticipated. Open yourself up to everything you deserve, and do the inner work so you *start believing you deserve it all*.

You are worthy.

You are enough.

You are magic in living form.

Trust me, there's a Black Gypsy within, waiting for you to show up, and we can't wait to meet her or him.

What's Next?

Want to hear the song I played for Patrick during the Uber ride in Paris?

See a video of Regina and I getting stuck in the sand in Bahrain?

Watch me actually eating the poor little cricket?

What about a picture of the owl?

Get free exclusive behind the scenes pictures, footage, a video chat with me,
plus be the first to find out about my upcoming group travel retreats.

Go to:

www.Black-Gypsy.com

How Can You Support?

1. TELL 3 FRIENDS

Tell 3 friends that love or dream of traveling about Black Gypsy.

Matter of fact, tell anyone you think will find it inspiring and entertaining.

Get a group together and discuss the book!

2. REVIEW ON AMAZON

Leave an authentic review on www.Amazon.com.

It will assist other readers that are searching, and will help the book out tremendously.

3. SHARE ON SOCIAL MEDIA

Share your favorite moments and pictures of the book on social media.

Hashtag #BlackGypsy

Follow to stay up to date with my upcoming adventures.

Instagram: @ShawnaSharee